CHINA

THE LAND AND THE PEOPLE

CW00839155

1 Girls in Kunming enjoying a break between school lessons.

2 Fields and factories on the outskirts of Kunming show a characteristic rural-urban blend.

CHINA
THE LAND AND THE PEOPLE

D.C. MONEY

Evans Brothers Limited

Revised Edition

iv

Published by Evans Brothers Limited
2A Portman Mansions, Chiltern Street, London W1M 1LE

Evans Brothers (Nigeria Publishers) Limited
PMB 5164, Jericho Road, Ibadan

Evans Brothers (Kenya) Limited
PO Box 44536, Nairobi

Text © D. C. Money 1990
Maps and diagrams by Oxford Illustrators © Evans
Brothers Limited 1984

All rights reserved. No part of this publication may be
reproduced, stored in a retrieval system, or transmitted, in
any form or by any means electronic, mechanical,
photocopying, recording or otherwise, without the prior
permission of Evans Brothers Limited.

First published 1984
Revised edition published 1990

The author expresses his gratitude to Dr. T. N. Chiu, Geography Dept.,
The University of Hong Kong for his helpful criticism.

Acknowledgements
AAA Photo 99, 190 BBC (McGeoffrey Sherlock) 114, 127, 130, 159; Sir
Peter Allen 100; British Museum 38; J Allen Cash 161, 162; Mary Evans
42; Richard & Sally Greenhill vR, viiiL, 30, 145; Robert Harding
(Associates) viiiL, 33, 69, 70, 73, 93, 97, 107, 115, 125; Alan Hutchinson
Library 47, 75, 118, 137; Dr Joseph Needham/CUP 31; ZEFA UK Ltd
viL, viiR, viiiR, ixL, ixR, 49, 96, 109, 133, 167, 178. All other pictures
by D. C. Money.

Printed in Hong Kong
ISBN 0 237 51164 9 (cased)
          51118 5 (limp)

Contents

Introduction

5 Modern China: Mineral Wealth and Industrial Growth *page 101*

Manufacturing Industries — Iron and Steel Industries — Non Ferrous Minerals — The Large Industrial Centres — The Distribution of Industrial Cities — The Northern Industrial Groups — Industrial Groups in Central China — The Special Economic Zones — Regional Industrial Centres — Manufacturing For, and By, the Rural Population — Craft Industries — Points to Consider.

6 Modern China: Improving the Communications *page 117*

The Waterways — The Roads — The Railways — Air Transport — Points to Consider.

x

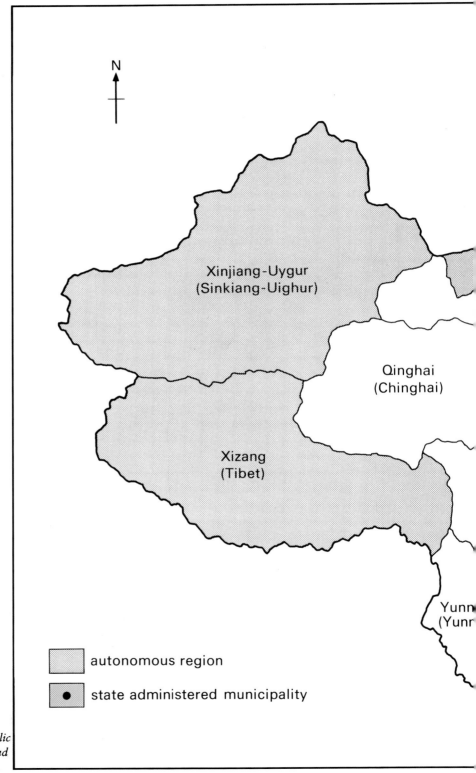

N

Xinjiang-Uygur
(Sinkiang-Uighur)

Qinghai
(Chinghai)

Xizang
(Tibet)

Yunn
(Yunn

autonomous region

state administered municipality

*3 The People's Republic
of China: Provinces and
Autonomous Regions.*

Proper Names

The Chinese have introduced a new romanised alphabet, known as *pinyin*, and have also simplified the form of pictograph writing to ensure that as many people as possible may quickly learn to read and write.

The new pinyin names are now used in maps and atlases, reference books and geographical magazines. But as the reader will continue to come across the old form of names (based on the Wade-Giles spelling system) in older books and atlases, alternative spellings are given in the text – with the pinyin names first. The alternatives are indicated where the name first appears, and then sufficiently often to make the reader familiar with each version.

In general, pinyin helps to produce a more realistic pronunciation. For example, the name of China's northern coal-mining city is more faithfully rendered as Datong, rather than by the former spelling – Tatung; and the name of the great leader as Mao Zedong, rather than Mao Tse-tung.

A guide to pronunciation is given below, and stresses several letters which may at first appear awkward, but which soon become familiar ('q' pronounced as 'ch' for example).

A guide to some of the pinyin names, and a list of alternative place names is given on p. 170. This also gives the meaning of some of the physical features described by place names, or indicated on maps: *jiang* (river), *shan* (mountain range), *dao* (island), and so on. Compass points form part of many names; there is *bei* (north) and *nan* (south) as in the northern and southern capital cities – Beijing and Nanjing; and also *xi* (west), in Xi jiang (the West River). The colour *huang* (yellow) occurs in many names: e.g. Huang He (Yellow River). In fact, the name and the word for river are often written as one (e.g. Huanghe and Xijiang): but here, where the reader is dealing with so many unfamiliar names, they are shown separated, as they are on most maps.

Pronunciation in the Alternative Systems

Pinyin

c – ts (as in *its*)
ch – ch (as in *chip*)
q – ch (as in *cheek*)
zh – j (as in *jump*)
o – aw (as in *law*)
u – oo (as in *too*)
e – e (as in *her*)
i – e (as in *eat*): or
i – ir (as in *sir*)
(after c,ch,r,sh,z,zh)
x – sh (as in *she*)
r – r (as in *right*): or
r – z (as in *azure*)

Traditional

ch' – ch (as in *chip*)
ch – j (as in *jeep*)
hs – sh (as in *she*)
p – b (as in *be*)
k – g (as in *go*)
t' – t (as in *top*)
t – d (as in *do*)
ts – z (as in *zero*)
o – aw (as in *law*)
j – (as r in pinyin)
i – e (as in *eat*): or
i – ir (as in *sir*)
(after c,ch,r,sh,z,zh)

4 China's landscapes reflect thousands of years of continuous development. Under this Sichuan ruler, Li Bing, part of the Min river was diverted into an irrigation system which is still being developed (p. 73).

Knowing About China

Many of us have very sketchy ideas about the People's Republic of China; yet there are very good reasons why we should get to know this great country. Eleven hundred million people, approximately a fifth of the world's population, live in China, and there are millions of Chinese in other countries in eastern Asia.

The country has a continuous history of civilised life going back thousands of years, so that modern China owes a lot to how people thought and behaved in those distant times. More than two thousand years ago, its people were thinking deeply about how they should conduct their lives and behave to one another. They were also practical people who worked out efficient ways of building houses and towns, making bronze implements and smelting and casting iron, and carefully diverting water to their fields.

Throughout the ages, the ideas of scholars and the practical ways of doing things have been handed down with the help of a pictorial method of writing (pictograph); this is in the form of characters which can be understood even by people who speak different languages.

The rulers and wealthy families often encouraged the scholars and helped artists to create fine painting and pottery. The administrators, chosen from the educated classes by examination, helped to keep the old traditions alive, even though, from time to time, invasions and revolutions set up new ruling families.

Yet, through the ages, China really depended on the toil and productivity of millions of peasant families and landless labourers. At times they lived in near-slavery; and, even at best, remained poor, compared with the other classes in society. In good times, their lives were brightened by everyday family pleasures and the bustling entertainments at local markets. But in times of drought or flood, or war, they usually suffered severely. Nevertheless, they, too, handed down through each generation their methods of cultivation, and their beliefs and superstitions. At all levels, the practical ways in which the people tackled natural hazards and outside interference helped to make them an independent people, proud of being Chinese, and able to look after their own affairs.

In some ways, however, China has been held back by her old traditions. In recent centuries, when the world population was already rapidly increasing, and European nations were developing modern industries and world-wide trade, the Chinese emperors and administrators tried to maintain the ancient ways of doing things, and sought to avoid outside influences. As their own population grew and grew, it was again the peasant farmers and landless labourers who suffered most. The nineteenth century brought revolutions and wars; and China was forced to accept interference by the 'Western' nations and by Russia and Japan. All of this meant that at the start of the twentieth century China was a weak country, with millions of impoverished people.

China continued to suffer greatly from the effects of foreign invasions and civil wars, until, after continuous internal struggles, the People's Republic was formed in 1949 and put the life of the Chinese people onto a new course, based on communist principles.

After such long periods of disruption, the government had first to provide the huge population with an acceptable standard of living. It concentrated on social reorganisation, with the help of limited improvements in technology. China is only beginning to adopt and expand the kind of industries and technologies used by the so-called 'developed' nations — the Western countries, Japan, the USA and USSR.

China is now rapidly developing economically, but is very different from most 'developing' countries. Since 1949 there have been, from time to time, abrupt changes in the methods of applying communist principles. Some strict policies, like those of the 'Cultural Revolution' (p. 47) dealt harshly with more liberal sections of the population, and undoubtedly hindered economic development. Yet, despite internal struggles and purges, China's communist system has succeeded in providing its peoples with basic needs — with adequate clothing, housing, medicine and education.

Compared with most nations, there has been little difference between the wealth of one person and another; although incomes varied between city and countryside and between types of employment. Now cash incentives to encourage productivity are creating wider variations. How

5 Many old, effective techniques have changed little. Here men build a wall by tamping down earth between pole-shuttering, as people did even before the time of Li Bing. Similar wide-handled tampers appear in ancient drawings.

China has brought this about in a relatively short time must be of particular interest to other 'developing countries'.

The government and communist party officials have aimed primarily at firm control over the huge population. They have sought to restrict its size and to raise living standards of the largely rural population by introducing a limited form of market economy. The pace of urban-industrial developments has been hampered by lack of technicians and dependence on foreign expertise and funding.

There are problems of providing higher education and suitable employment for the increasing number of young people, especially in the cities; most are directed to particular jobs. There are more serious problems in accomodating those who seek a more liberal democratic system and in allowing minority groups to have a say in their own affairs.

Vast numbers of government officials pass down the laws and regulations; part of a bureaucracy which adapts to all the twists and turns of policy. The insistence on using correct channels, and exactly observing detailed regulations, often hampers sensible changes at local levels. Many feel that recent rapid economic growth has stimulated corruption among officials.

The people owe much to those who led the Long March (p. 41) and developed a system which has brought material successes; but many now wish central controls to be relaxed and the higher officials to be democratically chosen and appointed. The horrific oppressions of 1989 must affect development as a whole, as foreign confidence in the country's stability is shaken.

China differs from other developing countries in being a major world power, with natural energy sources and nuclear energy projects to back up its huge manpower; but isolation from international trade and investment could prove a disastrous handicap to development.

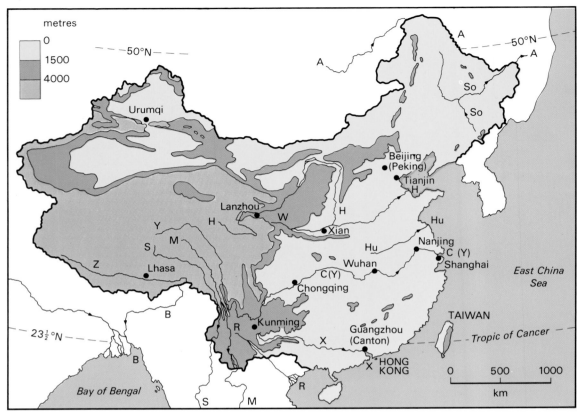

6 *A simplified relief map, showing the broad contrasts between highlands and lowlands and the trends of the main rivers (named in the text).*

A First Look at the Land and Its Peoples

China is a very large country indeed. It extends from the East China Sea to western Tibet, a distance of some 4000 kilometres; and it is about the same distance from the far north-east, at latitude 54°N, to the Vietnam border, which is in the tropics. This is roughly the whole width of Africa at the equator, or the entire length of Africa south of the equator. It is not surprising that there are striking contrasts in relief and climate in so large an area.

Its thousand million people include many minority groups besides the dominant 'Han' Chinese; together there are some 60–70 million who are not Chinese by origin. China's population is not evenly distributed over this huge country. Fig. 7 shows that the people are densely clustered in some areas, whereas other parts are

very sparsely populated indeed. Most of them are engaged in cultivating the land, and live in villages and towns in the rural areas; so that Fig. 7 virtually shows the distribution of the main cultivated areas, and emphasises how much of the country is not suitable for settled agriculture.

In general, most people live on the eastern lowlands; but there are also closely settled farmlands in other regions – on low plateaus and in the wide basins within the highlands. Much of western China is too high and rugged, with winters too cold and the growing season too short, for cultivation; and Fig. 22 shows that, in contrast to the more humid south and east, large parts of the north-west are so dry that any cultivation in valleys and basins depends mainly on irrigation, and there are immense deserts.

As one would expect, with a huge, increasing population and such densely populated regions,

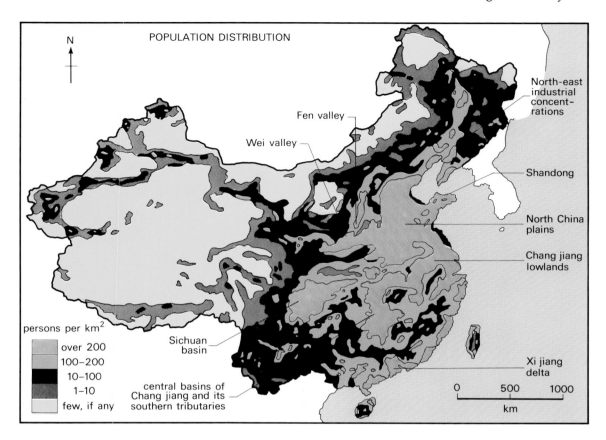

POPULATION DISTRIBUTION

North-east industrial concentrations

Fen valley

Wei valley

Shandong

North China plains

Chang jiang lowlands

Sichuan basin

Xi jiang delta

central basins of Chang jiang and its southern tributaries

persons per km^2
- over 200
- 100–200
- 10–100
- 1–10
- few, if any

0   500   1000
km

7 The population is concentrated on the rural lowlands; but there are dense clusters in such mineral-industrial regions as the north-east and Fen Valley, and in western oases with particular resources.

there are many large towns and cities. As an introduction, Fig. 6 includes just a few of the more important cities: it also shows the courses of the great rivers to indicate their location more precisely. These cities fall into several categories: the capital city – Beijing (Peking); three great city-ports – Shanghai, Guangzhou (Canton), Tianjin (Tientsin); some of the large regional cities – Xian (Sian), Lanzhou (Lanchow), Shenyang, Wuhan, Nanjing (Nanking), Chongqing (Chungking); and more remote regional centres – Urumqi (Urumchi) and Lhasa. It also shows two islands which the People's Republic regard as part of its nation – Taiwan, held by Nationalist Chinese (p. 159), and Hong Kong, whose New Territories, mostly on

the mainland, are leased by Britain until 1997 when the colony becomes part of the People's Republic of China (p. 152).

Now, in Part I, we look more closely at the natural features and conditions found in this immense country, and at their general influences on the vegetation and agriculture in its contrasting regions. Part II considers, briefly, the history of China's development over thousands of years, and shows how traditional ways of life have influenced the present population. Part III describes how the Chinese live today in the People's Republic, and considers their relationships with the rest of the world.

8 *Gullies in eroded loess indicate the huge quantity of fine material carried by the drainage system of the Huang He and its tributaries during summer. This is winter, with cart marks in the dust and an almost dry water channel; there are bare fields about the residual hill and on the gentler slopes.*

1 Natural Features and their Influences on Land Use

The Great Plateaus, Mountains and River Systems

The long rivers which rise in China's high western plateau and mountain ranges respond in many ways to patterns of highlands and lowlands which have been created over a period of a thousand million years and more. Fig. 9 shows that some rivers flow eastwards across the great plains of China to the Pacific – the Huang He, the Yangtze, known in its middle and lower courses as the Chang jiang, and the Xi (Si) river in the south. Other mighty rivers turn southwards – the Mekong through Indo-China, the Salween through Burma, the Zangbo (Tsangpo) flowing through the Himalayas to become the Brahmaputra. We can see how mountain ridges and rocky barriers affect the courses of these southward-flowing rivers in their curving valleys,

and create the huge right-angled bends of the Huang He in the north. Away to the north-east the Songhua jiang (Sungari river) is part of the drainage system of the Heilong jiang (Amur river), along which runs the boundary with the USSR.

Fig. 9 shows China's general physical structure. At first the tablelands, mountains, hills and lowlands hardly appear to form any regular pattern. But once we consider where and when ancient movements of the earth's crust slowly

9 *Notice the influence of the high relief and trends of the ranges on the drainage pattern, and the Qinling Shan divide between the river systems of the Huang He and Chang jiang. The lake basins in the central lowlands of the Chang jiang (Fig. 71) are not indicated here.*

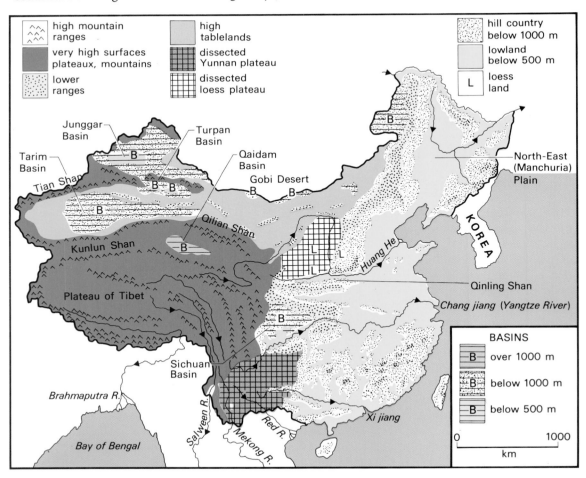

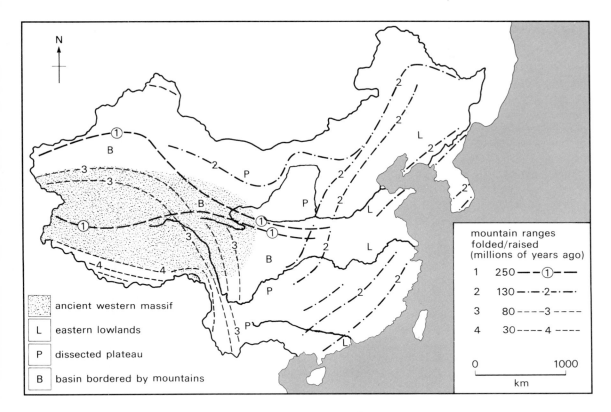

10 *High mountains were raised in different geological periods. Their trends influence China's landscapes today. Some are snow-capped ranges, with the world's highest peaks (4); but others (2) are now rugged, eroded hill country.*

raised the great plateaus and buckled up the mountain ranges, it becomes easier to follow the make-up of this immense country. Fig. 10 gives a much simplified view of the high tablelands and the lines of mountains which run through China. It shows where ancient rocks have been raised to form the plateau of Tibet; its surface is over 3500 m above sea-level, yet bordered on all sides by higher ranges. Hundreds of millions of years ago, earth movements formed the east–west lines of mountain ranges such as the Kunlun Shan (Fig. 9), whose snowy peaks rise to over 7000 m. These ancient movements also created the long ranges of the Tian Shan, shown as (1) in Fig. 10: (*shan* is the word for a mountain range).

The mountains called the Qinling Shan (Tsinling Shan), which extend towards China's eastern lowlands have particular significance. They are much lower, but separate the drainage systems of the Huang He and Chang jiang (Yangtze kiang). They also lie along the line of an important geographical divide, which marks the separation of the warmer, wetter south-east from the drier, colder winter climates of the north-west.

Another long period of earth movements caused further uplift of these ranges, and at the same time raised other mountains in eastern China along the NNE–SSW lines shown as (2) in Fig. 10. The latter have since been so eroded that they now form broken hill country, rather than mountains on the scale of those mentioned above. The valleys of the rivers which dissect them are important centres of settlement amid these eastern uplands.

A later period of mountain building created great sweeping ranges in the west (3). Finally, other movements raised the high snowy Himalayas, in which lie the boundaries between China and India (4). Fig. 9 shows how the lines of the mountain ranges uplifted during periods 3 and 4 have influenced the courses of the Mekong and Salween; and also that of the upper Yangtze, before river capture deflected its waters eastwards.

The Patterns of Highlands and Lowlands

The simplified view of China's topography in Fig. 6 enables us to see the country's separate physical regions more clearly. A structural simplification in Fig. 9 distinguishes between (a) the very high western tablelands and mountains; (b) the lower plateaus and basins which adjoin them; (c) a variety of broken uplands in eastern China; and (d) the lowlands close to sea-level, on which so many Chinese live.

In the north, the step-down from the high western tablelands to the lower plateaus is abrupt: from 4000 m to 1000 m. Parts of the large, dry inland basins (B) are less than 400 m above sea-level. Eastwards, there is a further fall to a lower tableland, sometimes called the 'Loess Plateau', for its surface is covered by thick deposits of fine dust (loess), which has been carried by winds from the interior and built into a soft rock. The surface has suffered badly from erosion (p. 7); but wherever water can be supplied, the loess lands prove to be very fertile. Loess also covers parts of the adjoining hill country to the east.

Further south, another large, enclosed fertile basin lies to the east of the western highlands – the basin of Sichuan (Szechwan), also known as the 'Red Basin' from the colour of its rocks and soils. The Chang jiang (Yangtze kiang) flows into and out of the southern part of this densely populated basin, most of which is wetter and milder than the dry loess lands. South again, is the higher plateau of Yunnan, which extends north-eastwards into Guizhou (Kweichow) province. Fault-bounded valleys in its surface contain many beautiful lakes, and the climate about Kunming, the Yunnan capital city, has been described as 'eternal spring'.

The next step-down is to the closely populated lowlands of eastern China. Fig. 9 shows how extensive these are. In central and southern China, they are separated by broken hill country. In fact, many people live in these rugged, partly mountainous regions, and cultivate the valleys and lower slopes. Nevertheless, the main lowlands are those of the great river basins and delta plains, built up of alluvial deposits.

Year after year, century after century, the summer floods of the Huang He have spread over a wide area, leaving, on retreat, thick alluvial

11 *Even among mountains, favourable locations are closely cultivated. Here, in western Sichuan, man-made terraces follow natural contours and the shape of wide river flats. Buffaloes plough recently flooded fields; bundles of rice seedlings are being made up in green nursery beds; and in the near fields seedlings are being planted in rows.*

deposits over the adjacent lowlands, and building up the wide plains of its ever-extending delta. The particles it carries are mostly derived from the loess lands, and the thick, muddy flow gives the Huang He its name – the Yellow river. The Chang jiang (Yangtze kiang) has also formed a wide delta. In its middle course the main river and its tributaries flow through a series of partly filled lake basins, which are among the most densely populated parts of China. The rivers flow into and out of lakes, and summer rains bring extensive flooding to these lowlands.

In the south, the Xi jiang (Si river) takes water from tributaries in the hill country south of the Chang jiang, from the Yunnan-Guizhou plateau, and from the southern, mountainous borderlands. In its lower course, rivers from the north also carry down materials which build out its broad delta. The sub-tropical climate helps to make this a rich agricultural region, where rice can be grown through the year (Fig. 26).

Far away to the north-east are very different lowlands – once called the Manchurian Plain. This is, in fact, a low rolling landscape, bordered by mountains, with extremes of temperature, especially in the north. In the southern part, rivers flow to the Gulf of Bohai (Pohai), but a gentle divide causes the northern parts to be drained by the Songhua (Sungari) and its tributaries towards the Heilong jiang (Amur river).

Three Great Rivers

Today, as throughout its history, China's very existence depends on the control and use of the waters of the major rivers, and on the soils formed from their deposits. Now that we have seen where the rivers flow, we will follow in more detail the courses of the Huang He, Chang jiang (Yangtze kiang), and Xi jiang; for the nature of each river, its valley, and the surrounding countryside changes from source to mouth, as do the uses made of the river waters.

The Huang He (Hwang Ho)

The characteristics of this great river, which receives water from an area bigger than France, vary considerably as it follows a course of some 5500 km, from its high source in Qinghai (Tsinghai) province to its delta in the Gulf of Bohai. It rises 4300 m up in high mountains, and flows eastwards and northwards, rushing through deep gorges and cutting through the snowy ranges of the Qilian Shan, where its energy is converted to electricity in two great multi-purpose dams (Fig. 108). On emerging, the river becomes wider and shallower as it winds its way northwards,

guided by the western edge of the plateau of Nei Mongol (Inner Mongolia), and flows across the very dry lands of the Ordos region.

Great bends occur where in the north it meets a line of mountains and turns eastwards and, again, where it meets the NNE–SSW ranges (shown as (2) in Fig. 10) and flows southwards to where the Qinling Shan guides the eastward course of the river Wei and governs the direction taken by the Huang He shortly after the rivers join.

The Huang He and its northern tributaries cut deep into the soft loess and acquire a huge load of yellow silt. The Wei and its tributaries also carry heavy loads of silt to the main river. It was in this fertile part of China that ancient civilisations flourished (p. 30), with the capital city, Chang-an, in the Wei valley, where modern Xian (Sian) now stands.

After receiving the waters of the Wei, the Huang He cuts through the barrier of the north–south ranges and the valley narrows. Here, at Sanmen, the Chinese have built another great dam. Below this, the river flows across wide plains which have been created by the immense amount of silt and sands it has carried down and dropped into a sea-filled trough. Over many thousands of years this lowland has been built up and extended eastwards to form much of the present North China Plain. Recent observations show how the river could do this: for over a period of two years the Huang He has dropped so much material at its

12 *This simplified relief map shows the present course of the Huang He and two river valleys, the Wei and the Fen, which have a long history of settlement.*

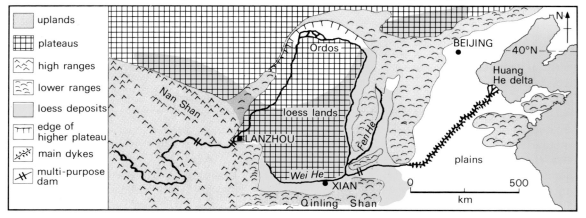

mouth that the coast has been extended 10 km seaward along a 60 km front.

In the dry winter months, the river fills only part of its shallow meandering channel. But summer rains can increase its flow a hundredfold, allowing it to carry an enormous load of silt. Vast flooding has occurred in the past, and within recorded history the Huang He has drowned millions of the people who have farmed the fertile soils. As the flow slackens, the river leaves much silt on its bed. Despite scouring by the summer currents, this has continuously raised the level of the bed, so that for hundreds of kilometres the river flows high above the surrounding countryside. Through the ages, dykes have been built to try to contain the flood waters; but from time to time breaches have caused such disasters that the Yellow river has also become known as 'China's sorrow'. Today, modern methods of strengthening the dykes are proving successful; and, even more important, the floods are being controlled by multi-purpose dams, like that at Sanmen, and by smaller dams on the tributaries.

Vast areas are threatened by flooding. Centuries ago, natural breaching of the dykes diverted the river from an outlet near its present mouth to flow hundreds of kilometres southwards and pour into the sea south of the Shandong (Shantung) Peninsula. In 1851 the river turned north again and flowed to the Gulf of Bohai. The dykes were strengthened; but in 1938 they were deliberately broken to try to stem the Japanese advance (p. 42), and hundreds of thousands perished. In 1947 the river was once again diverted to the north. Despite all these disasters, hundreds of millions of people continue to live on the plains and, like their ancestors, take advantage of the fertility of the alluvial soils, which are further enriched by fine wind-blown loess from the west.

The Chang Jiang (Yangtze Kiang)

The waters draining to this huge river, some 6380 km long, come from an area more than twice the size of the Huang He's catchment. Guided by mountains, it follows a southwards course from the high plateaus of Qinghai and into Tibet. Here it has cut narrow gorges, over a thousand metres deep, and further south its un-navigable torrents race below steep, forested valley sides. These valleys become hot in summer, for the river almost reaches the tropics before, as a result of a series of river captures, it zig-zags its way north-eastwards. Here, too, there are deep valleys where it breaks through the mountains into the enclosed basin of Sichuan (Szechwan). The name 'Sichuan' refers to four rivers which bring water from the north into the Chang jiang, as it flows in the trench it has cut in the southern part of the basin.

Leaving the basin, the river again cascades eastwards through long gorges cut into limestone

13 A simple map which shows the main physical features influencing settlement and development in the Chang jiang system. A gentle divide separates the Chang jiang and Huai He basins.

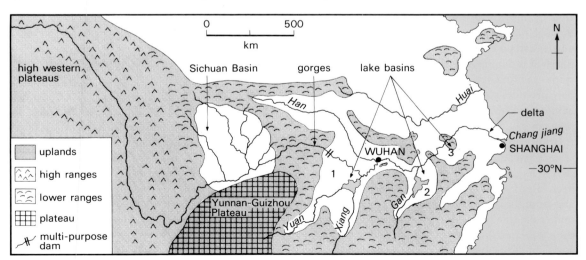

14 Here at Chongqing the already wide Chang jiang and the Jialing, which joins it from the left, flow between steep hillsides: even here, the brown, muddy colour shows the heavy load of fine material carried by the rivers. People disembark from the ferry boats.

hills, before emerging near Yichang (Ichang). For thousands of years, men have hauled junks up-river against the turbulent waters which rush through this long passage. Now small motor vessels can power their way up-stream, and where the river is dammed at the lower end of the gorges, ships are lifted in locks. Here the huge Gezhou dam provides electric energy (p. 97), and to some extent controls flooding on the lowlands further east.

Below the gorges, the Chang jiang drops to a series of swampy plains which form the middle part of its course. Here great lakes have mostly been filled by deposits washed down from Sichuan and from the bordering highlands. There are numerous smaller lakes, some taking the waters of the southern tributaries, the Yuan, Xiang (Siang) and Gan (Kan), before they flow through to reach

the main river. The summer rains still cause widespread flooding in the lake basins. Dykes flank the fields and form a patchwork across the flat landscape. To help control the summer flooding, long dykes were built to enclose two huge shallow overflow reservoirs (Fig. 71); in winter when the water has subsided, the beds of these artificial basins can be cultivated: for winter, by contrast, is a time of shallow water, when sandbars hamper river shipping. Isolated hills rise above the lowlands; but below Wuhan the river cuts through two low ranges, so that there are really three separate plains, shown as 1–3 in Fig. 13.

Beyond the last of these ranges, the river has built its great delta. Here the close networks of distributary streams and man-made canals are used to drain the land, provide irrigation water, and act as waterways. Here, too, deposits rapidly extend the coastline, forming land which is reclaimed by progressive dyke building. Northwards, only a gentle divide separates the Chang jiang delta from the lowlands of the river Huai (Hwai).

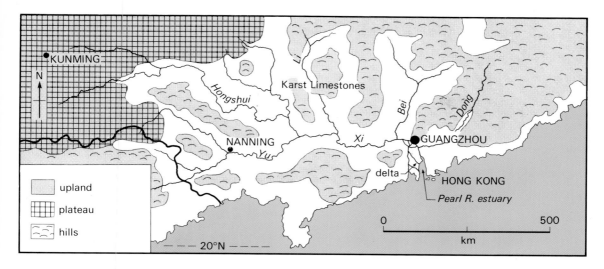

15 *The Xi jiang, with some of its main tributaries.*

The Xi Jiang (Si Kiang)

The highest tributaries of the Xi jiang rise on the Yunnan plateau, more than 2300 km from the sea. Most of the tributaries cut deeply into the landscape, and the plateau itself is very dissected. Their power potential is considerable, and there are plans for multiple dams on the Hongshui. The valley of the main river does not open out into middle plains as do those of the Huang He and Chang jiang; and the Yu, which joins it from the south has also cut into the landscape. Tributaries to the Yu drain the rugged, forested country of the Vietnam borderlands (Fig. 15).

The Li jiang, which joins the Xi from the north, flows between the spectacular, towering limestone blocks which make up most of the country about Guilin (Kweilin). This landscape of karst limestone provides little sediment, so it is a very clear river. But the Xi jiang itself carries a large load, as do the two rivers from the north and north-east which join it in its wide delta. Thousands of kilometres of tree-lined, dyked channels and canals thread through the flat river deposits. Near the mouth, the main channel is known as the Pearl river where it forms an estuary which has long been one of China's most important commercial waterways.

Points to Consider

1. There are clear patterns in China's physical structure. These are due to long-separated periods of mountain building, erosion and deposition.
2. Ancient earth movements have guided the lines of ranges and the courses of rivers, and created broad surfaces at different altitudes.
3. The main rivers show abrupt changes in direction, for various reasons.
4. China's geological structure affects present settlement, partly through mineral distribution, and, indirectly, by modifying the climate, soils and vegetation.
5. Young surface deposits, both wind-borne and water-deposited, are of immense value to the people of China.
6. Loess and alluvium, with particles derived from various sources, provide plants with a variety of nutrients.
7. China's rivers, their volume and their load, vary considerably with the seasons and with the distance from their source.
8. The load carried varies not only with the width and depth of the river channel and the gradient of the bed, but also with the surface rocks over which the river and its tributaries flow.
9. The lake basins of central China are some of the most closely settled areas.
10. Lowland lakes are usually fairly rapidly reduced by in-filling.

16 The clear waters of the Li jiang flow between sheer, rounded hills which are remnants of huge masses of weathered and eroded limestone, and on to join the Xi jiang. This is part of the karst country about Guilin.

Climates of the Different Parts of China

The glaciers of the high, snowy mountains, the dusty deserts of the north-west, the fields of spring wheat in the loess lands, and the rain rattling sugar cane in the Xi delta are just a few pointers to the great variety of climates in this huge country. Yet each of these different climates is affected by the location of China itself. It forms the eastern part of a large landmass, whose seasonal temperatures reflect 'continental' influences and whose surface can provide very little moisture; whereas eastwards are the seas and ocean, which supply moisture and exchange energy with the air above, so that winds from the sea can bring cloud and rain and modify the temperature.

Monsoon Effects: Seasonal Contrasts

During winter, the northern and central parts of the Asian continent receive little heat from the sun. Thus, as the surface continues to radiate heat into space, it becomes colder and colder, and chills the air in contact with it. This cold, dense airmass sinks and builds up a pressure so high that the air flows outwards from the interior. These outblowing winds particularly affect western and northern China. Here the winters are bitterly cold, and at times the air is full of dust from the deserts and loess lands. Occasionally, there are lulls in this eastwards airflow, which allow slightly warmer, moister air from the sea to move into northern parts of the country, and may cause snow; but such air seldom penetrates far inland.

South of the line of the Qinling divide (p. 9) conditions are rather milder and cloudier. But here, too, cold air occasionally surges eastwards, and as it clashes with the warmer, moister air, brings spells of cold, wet winter weather to parts of southern China. Figs. 17 and 18 emphasise the contrasts in winter between northern and southern China.

In summer, the land surfaces in the centre of the continent become hot, and are far from the cooling influences of oceanic air. As air rises from the heated surface, the high pressures of winter are replaced by low pressure during summer. Fig. 20 shows that, in general, the cold, dry north and north-westerly winter winds give way to warm, moist air moving in from the south and south-east. This reversal of wind direction is part of the east Asian monsoon with air flowing clockwise about the continental low pressure system.

17 *Early March sunshine near Simao in south-west Yunnan. Water buffaloes plough recently flooded fields, where white ducks are swimming. Tall, graceful bamboos surround the village on its promontory.*

18 *A March snowfall covers the small fields about a Shanxi village, west of Taiyuan, and the houses with their many chimneys. Here the trees are still bare.*

By May, most of southern China has become hot and humid, with rain brought by the southerly winds. Winds from the south-west also bring moisture into southern China. These are part of the inflowing monsoon air which crosses south-east Asia. During the following weeks, these conditions move northwards over the Chang jiang valley. The rain is not continuous; but frequent storms develop and can bring very intense rainfall where the moist airmass clashes with the continental air. Even the interior is affected by the inflow of moister air, though the effects of the

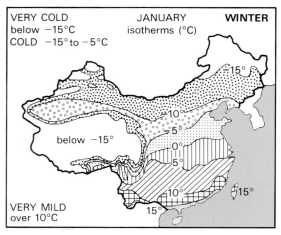

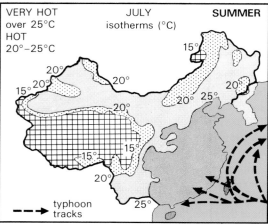

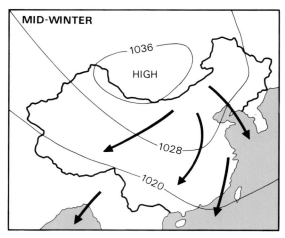

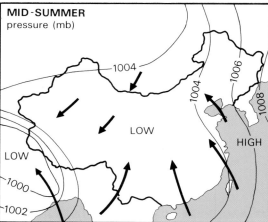

19 Mid-winter conditions, with a flow of bitterly cold air from the north-western interior. Disturbances can occur when surges of cold air meet the warmer, moister air in southern China.

20 Mid-summer, when very warm, moist air sweeps over southern China from the eastern ocean and from south-east Asia.

monsoon tend to become less with distance from the coast. However, where barriers, such as hills, plateau edges, and mountain ranges cause the air to rise, part of its moisture condenses and gives rain. Snow falls on the really high mountains. By July, occasional heavy storms affect the loess lands, and though, on average, there is a far lower rainfall than in the southern and eastern parts of the country, some years may be particularly wet, others very dry.

The Extent of the Dry Lands

Fig. 22 shows how the rainfall decreases away from the south and east. This simplified map emphasises the trends, and shows that much of the country is very dry indeed, especially in the north and west. There are many parts of China where the soils are fertile and summer temperatures high, yet crops can only be grown by irrigation.

This gives a general picture of the wet and dry parts of the country, but even more detailed rainfall maps do not necessarily give a correct impression of soil moisture. They may show that higher ground facing the wet monsoon winds receive more rainfall than adjacent, sheltered lowlands: but, of course, water runs readily from steep slopes and may accumulate in lowlands: and though slopes facing south may receive more rain, they are also sunnier than those facing north; so that, with a higher evaporation rate, they may, in fact, have drier soils. Also, of course, where the temperatures are low, and evaporation rates small, even a little precipitation may remain in the soil for a long time.

The Annual Range of Temperature

It is important, therefore, to consider exactly what a map can show. Because air temperature falls with altitude, maps of the *actual* mean temperatures (Figs. 19 and 20) allow contrasts between highland and lowland to stand out clearly. Yet these maps hide the overall effects of winds blowing from the land or sea and of the

sun's elevation at different latitudes. Those in Fig. 23 point to these influences by showing, by calculation, what the air temperatures might be at sea-level. These clearly show progressive differences between north and south and between the coastlands and interior. But remember that the

21 There are obvious contrasts in precipitation in winter and summer and between the south-east and far interior; but these average figures mask considerable variations from year to year.

22 Once again this is mean precipitation, and in many parts of China the amounts vary a great deal from year to year.

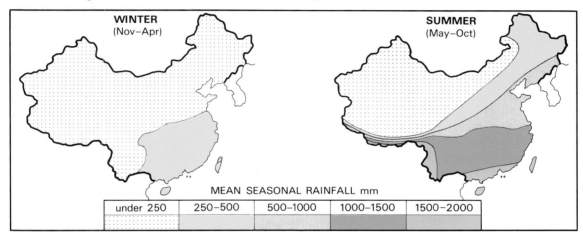

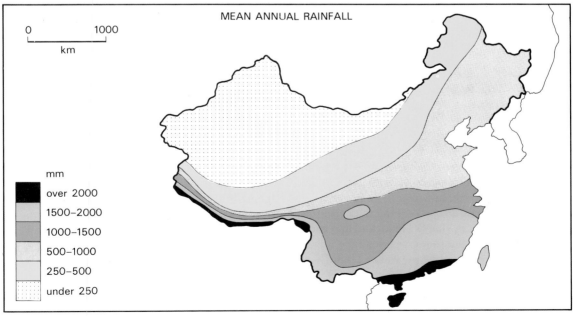

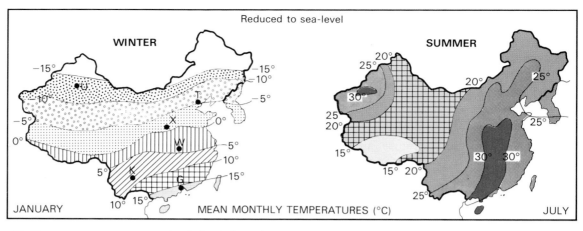

23 *Mean temperatures as at sea-level; they help to show influences other than altitude.*

actual winter temperatures on the Tibetan plateau, and high on the slopes of the Himalayas, are far below these *average* sea-level figures; even in the lower desert basins the actual air temperatures may fall to −25°C.

The winter isotherms in Fig. 23 reflect the facts that the sun's elevation and the number of daylight hours vary considerably between China's northern and southern borders. Seasonal changes are emphasised by the east–west trend of the isotherms in winter and the north–south trend in summer. It is also apparent that under the influence of warm monsoon air temperatures in summer vary far less between one part of China and another than they do in winter.

Mean climatic figures for places in different parts of China are shown on p. 169, and those plotted in Fig. 24 provide a ready comparison of climatic conditions in contrasting regions. All these maps and figures emphasise the large annual range of temperature in the north and interior.

How People Respond to Conditions

While the maps and average figures tell us a great deal, the way people react to the actual conditions completes the picture. In winter in Beijing (Peking) the people wear padded jackets and thick trousers. The jackets are often blue or khaki, and may look uniform and drab, but they give essential protection. Many women now wear a brightly coloured tunic over their jacket. The air feels sharp and raw and is often full of dust, so that gauze masks are used to cover the mouth and nose, as a protection as well as to prevent colds spreading. Women often use colourful nylon neckerchiefs to cover their face.

In summer the girls wear light blouses or tunics, usually with trousers, though many of them now put on light one-piece dresses or skirts. The afternoon temperature can approach 40°C and the mid-summer humidity is high, so that the cooler evenings are a time of great activity in the small streets about the city centre. Page 27 describes how the summer and winter climates affect people's lives in other parts of China, and the scenes in Figs. 90 and 121 speak for themselves.

Unreliable Rainfall

People farming the drier parts of the country not only have to cope with a small annual rainfall, but with its unreliability. In some years there is far less than the average, in others far more. Here, too, the rain which falls in summer storms is often heavy enough to wash away loose, dry soil and cause erosion. Great care must be taken to provide irrigation water, and to terrace the fields, for this controls the storm water run-off, retains as much water as possible, and holds back the soil.

The southern and eastern parts of the country have a more reliable rainfall, though even here there can be much variation between one year and the next. Occasionally, the coastlands of south-east China are affected by a tropical cyclone (typhoon). These generally move in from the Pacific and can do much damage, for the winds about their centre may be strong enough to uproot trees and destroy buildings. They bring torrential rain; sometimes as much as 500mm in a day.

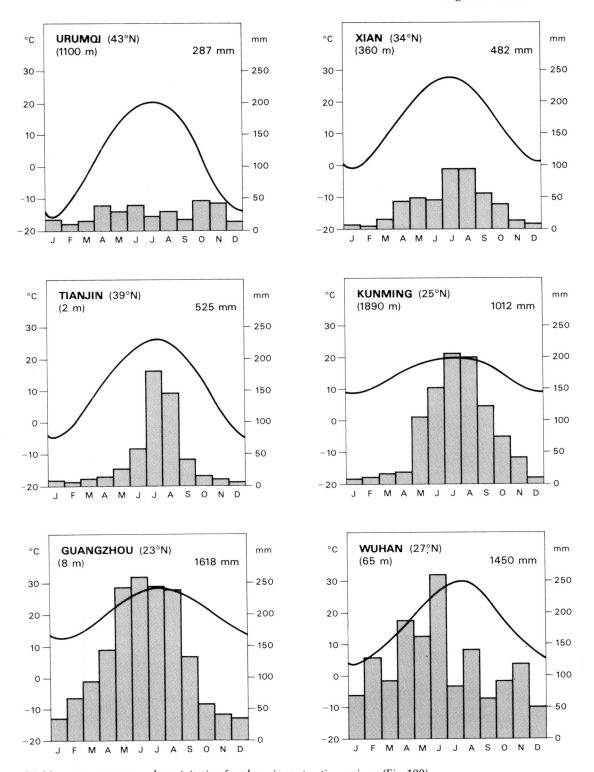

24 *Mean temperatures and precipitation for places in contrasting regions. (Fig. 199).*

General Points about the Climate

1 In all parts of China most rain falls in summer; but the amounts received vary greatly between one part of the country and another.

2 The south-eastern parts have most rainfall, with rainy periods in winter as well as summer. The summer typhoons may cause damage.

3 The rainfall is particularly unreliable in the drier lands.

4 High lands facing the winds tend to have more rainfall than adjacent sheltered valleys and basins, which can be much drier.

5 Evaporation from south-facing slopes can be much greater than from the north-facing slopes, causing differences in vegetation and crops grown on the two sides.

6 The inner parts of China have large annual temperature ranges, with hot summers and very cold winters. Such conditions extend to the north-east of the country. Yet, sinking, warming air can keep some inland basins milder in winter than one might expect – as in the Sichuan basin and those below the mountains of Xinjiang.

7 The air temperature of any place depends on its height above sea-level; yet while the *air* may remain cool in summer in high places, like the Tibetan plateau, the direct heat of the sun on the *surface* rocks, soils and crops can be intense, for the air is thin at these altitudes.

8 Daylight hours and the angle of the sun above the horizon at noon vary considerably between the far north and extreme south.

How Climate Affects the Vegetation and Crop Production

Most of the high western tablelands and mountains have an alpine vegetation, though this varies with height and with the direction the slopes face. Sparse grassland may extend up the sunnier, drier south-facing slopes, whereas the cooler, moister north slopes may be well grassed or bear coniferous trees. Coniferous forest is well developed in the wetter south-eastern highlands of Tibet; and quite thick forests remain in the deep river-valleys of the eastern parts of these highlands.

In north-west China the dry basins have only sparse drought-resisting vegetation, with patches of salt-tolerant shrubs; but many of the surrounding mountains have good high-level pastures. As Fig. 25 shows, wide stretches of dry grassland extend over a belt stretching across northern China, with grassy steppe on the lowlands of the north-east (Manchuria).

The loess lands have porous soils, and the drier parts support grassy scrub; yet their moister eastern and south-eastern parts were probably tree-covered, for much of the North China Plain once bore deciduous woodland, with mixed forest in the hills to the north. South of this, both coniferous and broad-leaved deciduous forest occur on parts of the Qinling (Tsinling) range, and the hills within and about the Sichuan basin have a great variety of trees, varying with the altitude, shelter and slope. This variety is also seen in the broad-leaved evergreen forests of southern China, where tall bamboos are a feature of the hillsides and valleys alike, and there are many pines.

However, China's natural vegetation has been drastically modified. People have been using the forests for firewood and timber, and clearing the

---

Further Points to Consider

1 Two monsoon systems affect China's climates – that of eastern-central Asia and that of India and south-east Asia.

2 In a country with so many different regions, climatic averages can be very misleading.

3 The climate of a particular area varies with its latitude, altitude, and distance from the sea; and also with local conditions of aspect and shelter from, or exposure to, seasonal winds.

4 Unreliable, erratic rainfall is apt to cause particularly serious erosion.

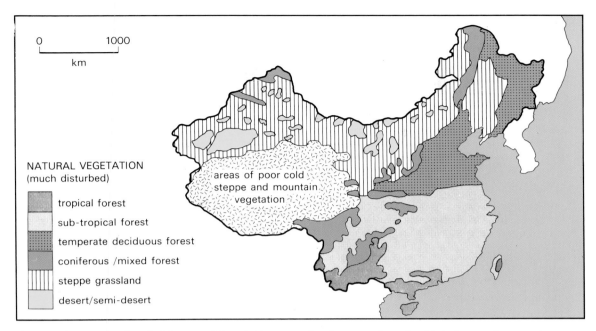

25 *Broad zones are identified, but people's activities over thousands of years have greatly modified the vegetation.*

land for crops and grazing for thousands of years. The moister parts of the loess lands may once have borne trees and shrubs and herbs, but this cover has been almost completely removed. The present landscape is made up of terraced fields and villages, with walls and roads. Many of the slopes, no longer protected by vegetation, have been deeply gullied by storm water, but are now covered with thousands of young trees. Page 147 describes plans for large-scale reafforestation.

Even in the more remote south-west, the sub-tropical hill forests show the effects of shifting cultivation. Instead of tall forest, the hillsides bear a patchwork of farmland and areas where abandoned fields are now covered with shrubs, bamboos and secondary woodland.

As with the natural vegetation, the type of plants which can be cultivated vary with altitude and latitude. In the sub-tropics, people in the low valleys often grow rice, with bananas and sugar cane, and the nearby slopes bear rainforest and bamboos; in contrast the higher slopes may be covered with pines and heathy plants, and fields in the high valleys may be planted with temperate grains and oilseeds. There is a surprising variety of

land use, and much of it is due to the ways in which the local climate affects the vegetation and the crops in the various parts of China.

The Main Food Crops

In Fig. 26 the two thick lines make very broad, but significant geographical divisions. The one running roughly north to south divides the drier pastoral country from the moister cultivated lands. The other, running west to east, partly follows the Qinling divide (p. 9). This line separates the drier, cooler north, where the main food grains are wheat and millet, from the warmer, moister south, where rice is the main grain crop, as indicated in Fig. 26B. In fact, rice is grown over many areas north of this line and wheat to the south of it; and other crops are grown before or after the main food grain, or in fields alongside it. But the broad divisons in Fig. 26A give a good general picture.

The choice of crops and patterns of farming depend to a large extent on the climate. The warm, moist winters of the south-east allow two rice crops to be grown in a year (double cropping); one is harvested in early summer, the other in late summer and is then followed by a winter crop, such as groundnuts, beans or green fodder. Of course, this puts pressure on the land:

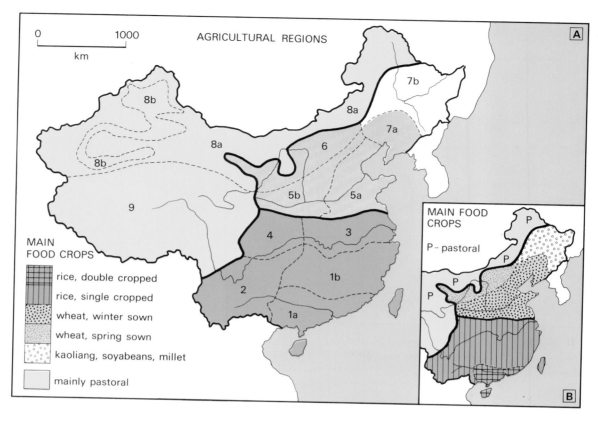

26 In A the heavy line separates mainly pastoral activities from arable farming; but important irrigated farmlands lie to the west of this divide. B shows the main food crops; but in many parts of central and southern China both rice and wheat are part of the annual crop rotation.

for, however fertile the soil, plant nutrients are lost when the crops are harvested, and must be replaced either by careful rotation which includes a leguminous crop (to replace nitrogen), or by the addition of natural or artificial fertilisers, to maintain the crop yields.

Some parts of the lowlands amid the southern and eastern hill country favour double cropping, but there is usually only a single summer rice crop, with, perhaps, sweet potatoes or other grains grown alongside. During the winter the temperatures allow oilseeds, such as rape, and various fodder crops to be grown. Much depends on altitude, slope and the availability of water.

Northwards from the Chang jiang (Yangtze kiang) delta, rice remains an important crop; but where spring and autumn frosts restrict the rice-growing season, it gives way to wheat. Over much of the North China Plain the wheat is planted in autumn and harvested in May; it can then be followed by kaoliang (Chinese sorghum), millet, maize, soya beans or sweet potatoes.

In the drier cold-winter zone which lies between these productive wheatlands and the pastoral areas of the north-west, the hard spring wheat cannot be sown until the end of March. Here the rainfall is both low and erratic, so that the hardier millet is also widely grown, as an insurance against drought.

Away to the north-east, there is fairly high summer rainfall, which suits maize. Wheat is grown in the southern province, Liaoning, but further north the long cold winter and short growing-season make soya beans, kaoliang and millet more suitable crops for the fertile soils of these former grasslands.

These divisions give only a general idea of the seasonal foodcrops in the various parts of China, and there are many regional variations. For

27 This is February, with yellow rape on village lands near Yi Liang on the Yunnan plateau. Compare the tiled houses, amid the bamboos and tall eucalypts, with those in Fig. 18. The cart with three small horses is a local characteristic.

28 The village near Yi Liang seen in Fig. 27. By May the rape has been harvested and threshed, the fields flooded and ploughed by water buffaloes, and rice seed beds established.

29 Spring, with young leaves on the trees and wheat in the fields near Luoyang. The small pagoda was built in the sixth century AD and restored during the Song dynasty.

instance, rice is grown in some of the warmer southern parts of the north-east; and over much of central China summer rice is followed by winter wheat. Again, these are only the main food grains; many other food and fodder plants, and commercial crops, such as cotton, are cultivated as well. Also, within these broad divisions there are hilly regions quite unsuitable for arable farming; while in the mountain lands and enclosed basins, different types of crops are grown at different heights on the slopes. Then, throughout China, there is intensive vegetable growing, sometimes in large fields, but also in small plots about the villages and in the cities; and almost everywhere pigs, chicken, ducks and fish are important sources of food.

Commercial Crops

Commercial crops are grown wherever possible, though exactly what is grown depends on climate, soils, and government policy (p. 53). The north-east is particularly suitable for soya beans, which are converted into oil, fodder cake, and hundreds of food products, including soy flour and milk substitutes. Cotton is widely grown: it is particularly important in the middle and lower parts of the Huang He and Chang jiang valleys and in Shandong, but is also a valuable crop in the irrigated lands far to the west. Tea grows best in the moist hill country of the south-east and central China. Rubber is mostly planted on the tropical Hainan island, but also, in rather cooler conditions, on hills in the far south-west. There are many other commercial crops, such as fibres, fruits, other tree products and mulberries. The following summary of China's agricultural regions, as indicated in Fig. 26, gives an idea of the conditions which favour particular rural activities.

The Agricultural Regions of China

The ways in which people strive to make the most of the land in different parts of the country are described in Part III. The blend of state control and private enterprise is officially the same: but as conditions vary so much from one part of the country to another that there is no such thing as 'typical Chinese farming'.

Consider a day in March. In the northern loess lands the trees are still leafless. People, wearing padded jackets to keep out the bitter wind, are harnessing horses to harrow the light grey-brown soils on the terraced slopes. Yet on the river flats in Yunnan, in the far south-west, farmers wearing thin shirts urge their water buffaloes through sunlit, flooded paddy fields, so that their ploughs can break up the heavy clods of earth, ready for the early rice crop. Their fields are bordered by banana plantations and clumps of sugar cane, and the green, forested hills are feathery with tall curving bamboos.

Even within one region, the whole agricultural scene can change in a short distance. A few hours by road may take you from the heat of those south-western paddy fields to cooler, higher valleys, bright with fields of yellow rape, and overlooked by hillsides covered with coniferous trees. China is a country of great variety. This is illustrated by the many agricultural regions shown in Fig. 26, and described below, with a brief summary of their climates.

1a Tropical and sub-tropical temperatures, with a 12-month growing season. Most rain falls in summer and is often heavy. Two spring and summer rice crops are followed by a winter crop of beans, or groundnuts, or green fodder, or wheat. Much fertiliser is needed: sometimes groundnuts are planted in alternate rows with sugar cane, to add nitrogen to the soil. There is a variety of fruits – bananas, mangoes, citrus, lichees and melons, with pineapples on hillsides.

1b High summer temperatures, with great humidity and much rainfall. There is some double rice cropping; but there is generally one summer rice crop; and in other fields there may be maize or sweet potatoes; these are followed in winter by peas, beans, rape and green fodder. Well-drained hill slopes are cultivated, if the soil is deep enough. There is much tea growing. Tree crops include mulberries (their leaves fed to silk worms), and tung (whose seeds provide vegetable oil). Bamboo and timber come from hill forests.

2 Hot moist summers; and during the mild winters there is some rain on the southern mountains and lowlands. There is a long growing period. The Yunnan plateau has cooler summers than the lowlands and a warm, dry winter. A single summer rice crop may be followed by winter rape, barley or beans. Tea, tobacco and cotton are cultivated as commercial crops. In the hotter south-west, bananas, papayas and sugar cane are grown, with rubber on the hillsides.

3 Hot summers: frosts occur until late spring and begin in late autumn. There are large areas of flat land with alluvial soils, which support a single summer rice crop, together with sweet potatoes, groundnuts and sesame (for oilseeds). In winter these may be followed by wheat, barley, rape, peas, beans or fodder crops. Cotton is an important commercial crop, and also ramie, which is used to make a Chinese equivalent of linen.

4 The Sichuan basin has an 11-month growing period. Rice is cultivated on the lowlands and terraced hillsides, and irrigation allows a double crop in some areas. Wheat and maize are grown in the uplands in the north and west. There is a great variety of crops, which vary with altitude as well as the seasons: they include sugar cane, tobacco, ramie, cotton and both sub-tropical and temperate fruits. Mulberry leaves feed silkworms and vegetable oils come from rape, groundnuts, sesame and tung trees.

5a The flat North China Plain with its alluvial deposits has hot moist summers, but cold winters, and a shorter growing season than further south. Occasionally, severe floods and droughts occur. Winter wheat, kaoliang, millet, barley, maize, soya beans and sweet potatoes are all grown, with a variety of vegetable crops. There is some rice growing, and cotton is important commercially.

5b Low to moderate, unreliable summer rainfall: cold winters. The loess-covered hill country and broken tablelands are terraced for winter wheat and millet. Other crops include maize, sugar beet, cotton, temperate fruits and pomegranates.

6 Colder and drier, with less reliable rainfall. Winter wheat gives way to spring wheat. There are also irrigated areas with cotton and tobacco. Kaoliang or millet is usually the second grain crop.

7a Long cold winters, but hot summers. A short growing season. Conditions vary considerably between north and south. The central parts produce soya beans, maize, barley, millet, sugar beet and temperate fruits. Cotton and groundnuts are also grown in the south, and rice in the warmer south-east.

7b The winters are severe; but state farms (p. 57) have been established and grow spring wheat and soya beans. In the north there is much rough pastoral land.

8a The dry north-western grasslands have sunny summers, and the eastward-facing mountain slopes receive moisture from the in-blowing summer winds. The winters are bitterly cold and dry. There are seasonal movements of sheep, goats, cattle and horses across the grasslands. But westwards the pastures become less productive.

8b Here the oases use water diverted from streams fed by snow-covered mountains, and also groundwater pumped to the surface to irrigate pastures and fields of spring wheat, maize, kaoliang, sugar beet and vegetables. It supplies large areas of cotton and sugar cane. There are good steppe pastures in the north-west.

9 The high Tibetan plateau is too dry and cold for much good pastureland, though there are nomadic yak herdsmen and some settlement on high mountain pastures fed by melting snows. There are lower, fertile areas in river valleys, like those about Lhasa, where grains, fruits and vegetables are grown, and cattle, sheep and yaks are pastured.

These brief notes show how China's agriculture varies with the physical conditions in regions which are described more fully in Part III. This looks at how China is tackling the problem of feeding a fifth of the world's population on a fifteenth of the world's arable land, and at the same time striving to maintain the fertility of the soils.

Points to Consider

1 Over most of China, the present vegetation bears little resemblance to that of the distant past.
2 Maps like Fig. 26B show a clear division between wheat- and rice-growing areas. In fact, these crops may follow one another seasonally; and pockets of wheat-growing may occur well within the rice areas, and vice-versa.
3 Sometimes a number of different grain crops are grown in an area as insurance.
4 Rotation to preserve soil qualities often governs the sequence of crops grown.
5 For climatic reasons, the value of land acquired for cultivation is apt to be greater for families in southern China than for those in the north.
6 Climate, plants and soils are inter-dependent. But so are other components of the living world. To prevent grain losses, there was a nation-wide campaign to kill off most of the birds. The resulting havoc to crops, caused by uncontrolled soil pests, was only one serious consequence.

2 China through the Ages

The Past and the Present

Knowing what happened in the past gives us a better understanding of Chinese ways of life and of China's attitude to the rest of the world. China has a long history of civilisation; and so much has been recorded, that to present a general picture of life over thousands of years, a great deal of historical interest has to be left out. What we can do is to select periods when developments took place which greatly affected the life of the people. We can look at practical advances in methods of building, controlling water, and farming, for example; and also see how, at certain times, thoughts put forward by scholars, like Confucius, were accepted, and when religious teachings, such as Buddhism, began to spread. We can place such advances during certain dynasties of emperors, just as we can the work of particular craftsmen and artists.

But, of course, millions of ordinary peasant families also passed down their knowledge and their ways of doing things: practical things like building a wall, and age-old customs, which have changed only slowly over the centuries. There have been great changes in recent years, yet journeying through China today one recognises scenes illustrated in centuries-old paintings and pottery designs. The Chinese people are making great efforts to develop a modern industrial socialist state; but China is still very much a rural country, and so much of the past influences the present and gives strength to the nation.

The Beginnings: States Develop in the North-West

Many thousands of years ago, groups of people, using stone implements, began to cultivate the light soils of the loess lands and the middle Huang He valley, territories which were later to become the 'heartland' of Chinese civilisation. Gradually, families came together to form small states, and walled settlements became common under a

30 The Great Wall with its watch towers running along the ridges of the Yanshan, north-west of Beijing. Its average height is nearly seven metres. This section was much restored during the Ming dynasty.

dynasty known as the Shang. Here people became particularly skilled in using bronze, and developed a form of writing carved into bone.

Nearly three thousand years ago a group of nomadic people, the Chou, overthrew the Shang and established a dynasty which dominated the other states for some eight hundred years; though, even so, there was much fighting between these small, scattered, almost independent kingdoms. Despite this, the total population of these lands increased ten-fold during this period, to about fifty million.

Ways of Life: Daoism (Taoism) and Confucianism

By now the people were using iron for their farm implements and weapons, and had developed large-scale water control systems to irrigate their fields. The individual states, with noble families at their head, were armed and fortified, and still very independent. Some built long walls to guard against attacks by groups of nomads from the north. Trade grew between their cities, and new settlements spread beyond the original heartland, southwards towards the middle Chang jiang and eastwards towards Mongolia.

There were long periods of settled life, when the richer families had the leisure to create, or commission, fine works of art or craft. There were great social differences between the noble families, the middle class officials able to use the pictograph Chinese characters for writing, the skilled potters and metal workers, the peasant families, and the merchants.

Scholars found time to consider how people should live together in society and behave towards each other to their best advantage. The thoughts and sayings of two of them have especially influenced the Chinese through the centuries, and still do today.

Lao Zi (Lao-tzu), who was born about 600 BC, considered that people, who were part of the natural world, should be free to organise themselves to act together for the good of all. He also saw that in the course of struggling to organise others, and through seeking power, people could lose their natural goodness. He suggested a Way (Dao) to live in harmony with

31 An almost timeless scene of city life in Kaifeng (Henan), when, in AD 1125, it was capital of the Northern Song – men with shoulder poles and horses with sacks surge past foodstalls and over the bridge.

nature by being loving, honest, seeking learning and being charitable. From such thoughts people later developed Daoism, as a form of religion.

About a hundred years later, Confucius, a wandering scholar, suggested how each group in society should behave. The rulers should be kind and sincere; the subjects loyal; the scholars honest in their thinking; and the young should respect their elders. In fact, strong, obedient family life, with reverence for ancestors, was already part of Chinese life, and remained so through the ages.

This kind of Confucian thinking, with everyone playing his proper role in society, was used later to maintain traditional customs and order in China, with people looking upward, through ranks of officials, to the emperor at the top, and through him only to the worship of heaven.

Two hundred years after Confucius, when the states were quarrelling and breaking away from the rule of the Chou dynasty, the scholar Mencius went further, and suggested that people had a duty to rebel against a wicked ruler.

The First Chinese Empire

Fighting increased among the states until, by 221 BC, the Qin (Chin) people, from the south-west, crushed the rest. Their ruler Qin Shi Huang Di, proclaimed himself the 'First Emperor', for, from the city of Chang-an (near present-day Xian), he came to rule over and administer a real empire, rather than simply controlling a group of other states. The name 'China' remains.

Shi Huang Di, like most strong rulers, did good things and bad things. He forced hundreds of thousands to labour on the immense task of linking, and then extending the old state walls. The result was a Great Wall which ran for some 2250 km from the north-western borderlands eastwards to the sea. Many thousands died while building it. Near Chang-an, he caused a great canal to be dug parallel to the Wei river, to control floods and supply water; and a road system to be built to link distant parts of the empire. His administrators standardised the axles of carts, to enable those from one state to fit the ruts in the roads of another state; and by creating common weights and measures, they enabled goods to be traded more efficiently. The emperor established governors over the states, and broke the power of their ruling families. But when scholars supported the families, he ordered the destruction of all scholarly writings.

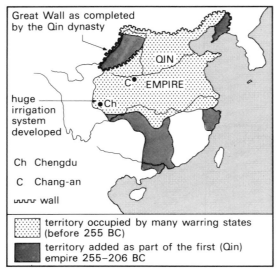

32 Separate states brought together under the Qin (Chin), from whom the name China *is derived, though the Chinese prefer to relate themselves to the Han.*

33 Part of the terra-cotta army of Qin Shi Huang Di which is being excavated from the loess to the east of Xian. The men once had metal weapons; archers with elaborate cross-bows guarded the flanks; and at some distance supporting stables and stores have been found.

The Empire Spreads Outwards Under the Han

During Shi Huang Di's reign, potters toiled to create a vast terra cotta army to accompany him to the next world. This has recently been unearthed near Xian. His successors were less able, and were soon defeated. Nevertheless, the things he had achieved allowed a period of united progress under the Han dynasty, which lasted from 206 BC to 220 AD.

Of course, we cannot follow all the political events of the next two thousand years, but the Han period deserves examination, for under their rule the Chinese settled far to the south, about the Xi river and in Indo-China. The northern Chinese and their descendants are still referred to as 'Han Chinese'. Their influence also extended westward, with trade routes north of the Tibetan plateau, through Afghanistan and Persia, to the Mediterranean and ancient Rome. Merchant linked with merchant along this 'Silk Route', as camels, mules, horses, and yaks carried silk to the west and brought back precious stones and metals.

In China there was a revival of education. The brush pen began to be used, not just on bamboo and wood, but on silk, and later on paper. Government officials were appointed by means of examinations. There were many practical advances. The magnetic compass was developed, a grid system used for mapping, and a seismograph constructed to locate earthquakes. Many large canals were linked together for irrigation and navigation, and rudders and paddle wheels were used on the boats. There was deep drilling for brine and natural gas. Medicine was studied, and treatment included acupuncture.

During this period, agriculture benefited from the large-scale irrigation works and dyke building, from the intensive application of fertilisers, the adoption of wheelbarrows and seed-drills, and the use of animal- and water-power for milling. But, even so, conditions of life varied with a person's position in society. Although the state expanded and prospered and large land-owners became rich, the poor peasant farmers were burdened by high taxation and were called-up to serve in the Han armies, which controlled the new territories. They were the first to suffer from the floods and droughts, which continued to devastate parts of China through the ages.

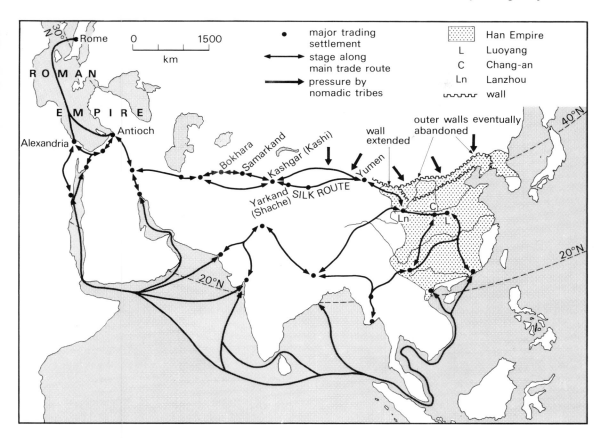

34 Merchants and goods usually moved in stages between the main trading settlements along these important trade routes between Europe, southern Asia and the Han empire.

Buddhism Arrives

Under the Han dynasty, men had travelled to India to collect holy Buddhist writings. When the Han dynasty broke into three separate kingdoms, Buddhism was officially recognised in the north, which was controlled by Tartars from central Asia, and was followed by large numbers of people. Despite these divisions, the Chinese ways of life continued, and now monasteries, temples and pagodas first formed part of the landscape. These became even more numerous under the Tang dynasty which followed, and which once more united China. The code of Confucius, and the control of everyday life by scholar-officials remained; yet both Buddhism and Daoism were accepted, and borrowed ideas and practices from each other.

35 Wall sculptures in a cave at Yungang, west of Datong. The caves here were first excavated and decorated during the fifth century AD, when the Northern Wei dynasty accepted Buddhism from southern Asia. Indian and Persian influences are seen in the smaller flanking figures.

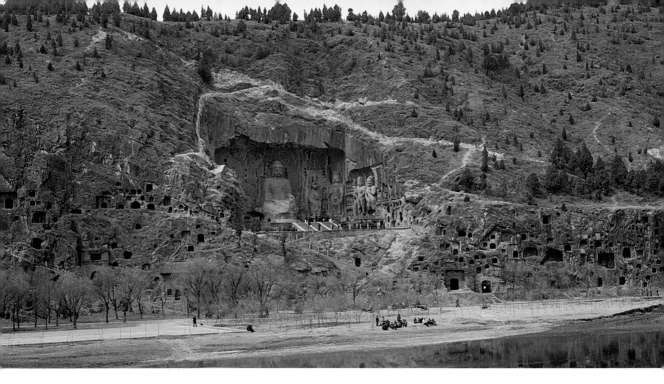

The Tang Dynasty: Commerce and Arts Flourish

An uprising had helped to establish the great and successful Tang dynasty, though before this progress had continued in many ways. For instance, a canal was built in eastern China to link the lower Chang jiang with the Huang He, so enabling grain to be carried northwards more easily.

The period under the Tang dynasty, from AD 618 to 907, was what has been called a 'Golden Age'. China was then the world's largest state, with a population of over 70 million, and organised by an educated civil service. By the eighth century, block-printing allowed text books and scrolls to be widely distributed. The poets and painters of this Chinese empire produced beautiful and lasting works.

Commerce flourished, and merchants flocked to the large walled cities, such as Chang-an (Xian), where Tartars, Tibetans, Arabs, Persians, and Koreans all traded in its markets. The lay-out of Chang-an was typical of these northern Chinese cities. Walls, with regularly spaced gates, which were locked at night, formed a rectangular barrier about streets arranged in a grid pattern. There were districts for different classes of people. Curved, tiled roofs covered the buildings – a characteristic which has remained throughout the centuries. The emperor reigned from an imperial

36 There are over a hundred thousand images of Buddha in these caves at Longmen, near Luoyang, seen across the river Yi: their decoration continued from the Northern Wei to Tang dynasties.

city, enclosed by walls. Markets, fields and parks broke up the street pattern. Fields for vegetable growing and parks with beautiful gardens are still a feature of Chinese cities – though, today, there may also be large areas of greenhouses for intensive cultivation.

The southern and central parts of China now had a large population, and supplied increasing amounts of rice to the north. The small market centres were growing into large towns. Flourishing commercial cities, such as Hangzhou (Hangchow), the southern capital, had spreading suburbs, and were more sprawling than the northern cities like Chang-an. After the end of the Tang dynasty, the population of the south continued to increase, and the rice-growing plains of the south-east became densely populated.

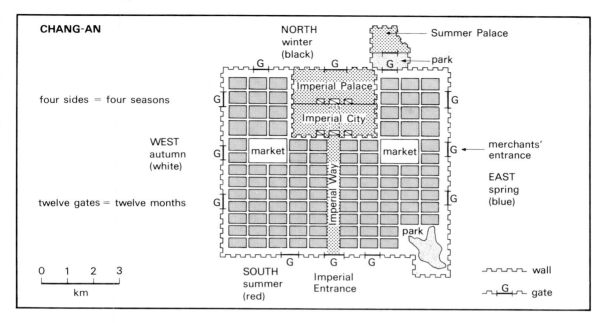

CHANG-AN

NORTH
winter
(black)

Summer Palace

park

four sides = four seasons

Imperial Palace

Imperial City

WEST
autumn
(white)

market

market

Imperial Way

merchants'
entrance

EAST
spring
(blue)

twelve gates = twelve months

park

0 1 2 3
km

SOUTH
summer
(red)

Imperial
Entrance

G — gate
wall

37 Chang-an at the time of the Tang dynasty, with its regular plan and ritual features: the walls related to the seasons, and gates for appropriate entries. The upper classes, with their own market and park, lived mainly in the east. Not all was housing; like Chinese cities today, it contained cultivated land.

The Song Period: Scientific Progress and Times of Hardship

There were upheavals after the break-up of the Tang empire, but trade continued during the Song (Sung) dynasty (AD 960–1279). Education became more widespread among the middle-class merchants and craftsmen. The emperors and nobility were, once again, patrons of scholars and artists and scientists, for there were many practical advances.

New devices led to the widespread use of water-powered machinery for pumping, drainage, threshing and milling, which helped the big landlords increase their wealth. As always, the hard-working, poor peasant farmers produced most of this wealth, and remained at the mercy of the estate owner. Many benefited from the progress made by wiser landlords; but large numbers lived in semi-slavery, as landless labourers.

There were further improvements in flood control and irrigation, which provided more land for cultivation. Fish were introduced to the

flooded ricefields, and not only provided valuable food, but also ate mosquito larvae, which helped to prevent malaria spreading. Lakes and village ponds are still stocked with fish, and are a great source of protein food in modern China.

38 The twelfth-century Song artist, Chang Tse-tuan, shows a town in Henan. Wheelwrights work while others relax beside the river, where sizeable boats are tied-up.

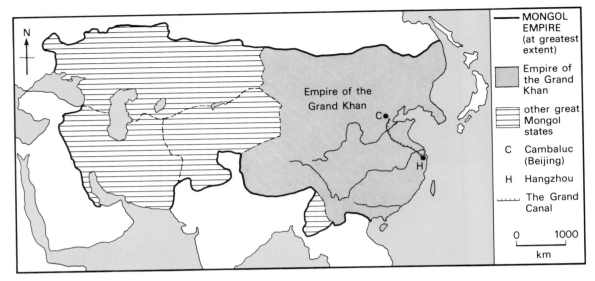

MONGOL
EMPIRE
(at greatest
extent)

Empire of
the Grand
Khan

other great
Mongol
states

C Cambaluc
(Beijing)

H Hangzhou

The Grand
Canal

0   1000
km

39 *Close relationships between the empire of the Grand Khan and the Mongol rulers controlling huge areas to the west allowed approved travellers the freedom of movement which brought many contacts between Europe and China.*

There was also progress in other directions. The demand for iron for farm implements, as well as for weapons, nails and coins, caused a great growth in iron ore mining and smelting in northern China. Charcoal was needed for this, and so there was rapid destruction of the northern woodlands, which, in view of the erratic climate, led to much erosion. Coal was also used at this time, though not to any great extent.

China Under the Mongols

During the thirteenth century, huge forces of nomadic Mongol horsemen, under Genghiz Khan, had dominated central Asia and the borderlands of southern and Western Europe: they also harassed western parts of China. By 1215, despite being faced by large numbers of Chinese, some with flame-throwers, the Mongols swept through the hills to the north of modern Beijing (Peking). They took control of northern China, and under Kublai Khan, who ruled from 1260–1294, built a great city, Cambaluc, where Beijing now stands. This was laid out in a regular pattern, as in old Chang-an.

Shortly after this they completed their conquest of central and southern China, and founded many walled cities there; so that the country was once more under a single ruler, of the Mongol (Yuan) dynasty. During the Mongol control of China and central Asia, many merchants, foreign representatives and missionaries travelled fairly freely from the West to visit the land they knew as Cathay (China). Western China, in particular, had a large Moslem population. Today, there are some twenty million Moslems in China, with concentrations in the western cities, such as Urumqi, Xian and Kunming.

Under the Mongols, large amounts of rice were sent to Cambaluc from the southern delta lands. Its movement was helped by the construction of the Grand Canal, which was extended northwards from the earlier link between the Chang jiang and Huang He. It has remained an artery of communications between north and south China for centuries, being deepened from time to time. Today, there are plans to develop it as part of an overall scheme for improved inland waterways (p. 119).

Eventually, there were rebellions in central and southern China, and in 1368 the Mongols were overthrown. The new Ming dynasty was established with its capital at Nanjing (Nanking); but in 1403 the Ming emperor and his court moved to Beijing (Peking).

Hardships for a Growing Population

The Ming dynasty not only tried to revive China after the Mongol occupation, but aimed to bring back something of the glories of the Tang and Song empires. The powerful and rich were favoured, and fine works in porcelain and painting produced. But the peasant population continued to be exploited, despite the considerable advances in agriculture which took place. Crops which had their origin in America, such as sweet potatoes, maize and groundnuts were introduced. Rice strains were improved and species with shorter growing periods allowed two rice crops a year in southern China. Partly because of this, the population increased from 80 million to 150 million during this period, so that the land had to support almost twice as many people.

Much of the wealth from the land went to rich landlords and corrupt officials, for the people were crippled by taxes. The Court had become backward-looking, and was bound up with the observance of pomp and old customs. In the end, these conditions, and the continued growth of population, led to serious famines and unrest. At the same time, Mongol and Manchu tribes were carrying out raids in the north-east. Manchus pressing south along the coast found weakening opposition from a disunited people.

40 An archway in the Forbidden City leads to the beautiful Dragon Screen, which typifies the splendours of the palace built under the Ming and restored during the Qing dynasty.

Manchus Found the Last (Qing) Dynasty

In 1644, the Manchus took Beijing and founded the Qing (Ching) dynasty. They expanded the Chinese empire northwards to the Heilong jiang (Amur river), and north-westwards to where the Russian empire was expanding. Yet, once again, China absorbed its conquerors. The Manchus soon became involved in the customs and observances handed down from the past. Officials, still appointed after examinations in Confucian ideas, were allowed to run things in traditional ways.

The population continued to soar, from about 160 million in 1700 to some 300 million by 1800 (Fig. 173). There were efforts to help the vast numbers of poor peasant farmers, and genuine concern by the long-reigning Manchu emperors. Yet local landlords continued to exploit the poor, and the emperors and their court kept China isolated from the rest of the world, and so lost the benefits of trade. The ruling classes maintained a typically Chinese attitude, feeling that they, at the centre of the world, with their unique culture, were self-sufficient, while beyond lay the uncultured barbarian peoples.

But the rest of the world now included great industrial-commercial nations, and soon 'Western' interference would change the course of Chinese history.

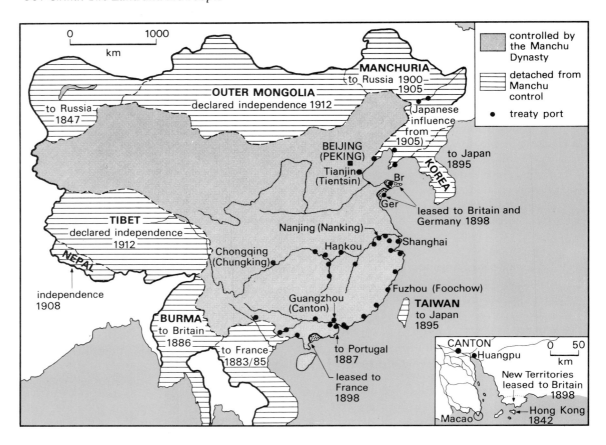

41 *A map which emphasises the extent of European interference in Manchu China during the late 19th and early 20th centuries.*

China and Western Influences

Under the Ming emperors, Chinese fleets had sailed south to Malacca and into the Indian Ocean, to Sri Lanka (Ceylon) and East Africa. Chinese merchants began to trade in Malacca and in the East Indian islands of Java and Sumatra. During the sixteenth century, Portuguese ships visited south-eastern ports of China, and in 1557 Portugal was allowed to set up a small trading colony on the Macao peninsula.

The Dutch established a base on the large island of Taiwan, but were ousted in 1683, when, for the first time, it became part of the Chinese empire. Luzon in the Philippines had been colonised by Spaniards and had already become an important trading base, to which many Chinese migrated.

European merchants were keen to trade with China, and during the eighteenth century ships of many nations faced the hazards of Japanese pirates to visit ports in southern China, especially Guangzhou (Canton), on the banks of the Pearl river, part of the Xi estuary. In 1757 the emperor decreed that all trade with China must pass through the 'factories' at Guangzhou, which were compounds leased from local landlords.

The emperor and court were, in fact, against trade with the West, and informed foreign officials that China lacked nothing and had no need of outside manufactures. Chinese traders at Guangzhou had to obtain conditions for trade from Beijing (Peking), which took many weeks.

However, the British, especially, had begun to make great profits by trading in opium, grown in India and other parts of the British Empire. In 1800, the emperor banned the import of this drug, which was harming the people and draining silver bullion from the country. The British persisted, and in 1839 Chinese officials burnt merchants'

42 The waterfront at Hankow (now part of Wuhan) in 1889, showing the European dominance of this treaty port so far inland, with the British flag flying.

stocks at Guangzhou. Fighting broke out when attempts were made to blockade British ships engaged in the trade; and during the 'Opium War' of 1840–42 the British occupied Hong Kong and attacked ports along the coast. In 1842 China was forced to negotiate the Treaty of Nanking, whereby Britain gained Hong Kong and the right to trade in the *treaty ports* – Guangzhou, Xiamen (Amoy), Fuzhou (Foochow), Ningbo (Ningpo) and Shanghai. Soon, France, the USA, Italy and Germany acquired similar rights.

Living conditions continued to be desperately poor for most of China's growing peasant population. Land shortages, high taxes and severe floods had brought misery to millions of Chinese, most of whom resented Manchu rule. In 1850 rebellion broke out in south-central China, and for fifteen years the people fought to overthrow Manchu domination. The uprising, known as the 'Taiping' rebellion – an abbreviation of the 'Heavenly Kingdom of Great Peace' promised by its leader – proved that peasants could wield power, even though the horrific number of twenty million people perished in the long struggle.

The European powers were involved in many

skirmishes. In 1856, the British fought the Manchu government over interference with commerce, and forced them to yield more trading rights and to make the opium trade legal. The rebellion had weakened the imperial army, and in 1860 the emperor fled from Beijing. The French and British sacked the Summer Palace; but then, preferring a weak Manchu rule to the unknown, the European powers helped the emperor to enforce a peasant surrender in 1864. They had gained new rights to open up China to foreign trade, and the numbers of treaty ports increased.

The influence of the Western nations was now strong. They could use the rivers and build railways. They divided parts of China into trading areas, where each nation had special influence. Thousands of missionaries came from Europe and America, many hoping to promote welfare as well as Christianity; they made many conversions but were distrusted by most of the people.

China's tributary state of Vietnam was lost to the French in 1885, and Upper Burma to the British in 1886. A dispute with Japan over Korea led to war in 1894, when China's fleet, with warships bought from the West, was disabled. In 1895 the victorious Japanese took Taiwan and other islands, and Korea became independent.

During the second half of the century, millions of Chinese emigrated, particularly from the south,

43 *French-style buildings in the former Foreign Concessions at Shamian island in Guangzhou (Canton). They have been converted into numerous flats.*

mainly to seek labouring jobs in south-east Asia, America and Australia. However, these latter countries soon restricted immigration.

In China there was, naturally, great anti-foreign feeling. In 1900, a society known as 'The Boxers', who called for people to destroy foreigners, and had killed many missionaries and converts, entered Beijing and set siege to the foreign legations. The old dowager empress, Ci Xi (Tz'u Hsi), who had been the power behind the Manchu throne since 1861, allowed soldiers to take over from the Boxers. The siege lasted 55 days, until an international force relieved the defenders. The foreign powers then took even firmer control, not only through the military, but by running banks, shipping, insurance, railways, and mining companies. The dowager empress died in 1908, and the powerless emperor was killed by intrigue, so that her two year-old nephew, Pu Yi, became the last emperor, until the Manchu dynasty ended in 1912.

The Chinese Republic is Created

Uprisings against the Manchus increased. In 1911 a Revolutionary Alliance Party helped a peasant revolt in Sichuan, and then backed a mutiny in Wuchang, now part of Wuhan, which enabled it to gain such control over central and southern China that the government had to negotiate with the rebels.

The Chinese Republic was proclaimed in January 1912 by Sun Yat-sen, who had long worked for the revolution. Yet he was soon replaced. The new president was a warlord, who aimed to become emperor; and, though he died in 1916, China was left in the hands of other powerful warlords, who controlled their own armies and levied taxes on local people. Sun Yat-sen's Nationalist revolutionary party, known as the Kuomintang (KMT) was banned.

As Germany was now at war in Europe, Japan promised China to remove the Germans from their Chinese concessions in Shandong, for China supported Britain, France and America. But, having done so, the Japanese remained there, and also demanded full control over mineral-rich

Manchuria, where they had industrial and commercial interests. Although Britain, France and the USA had gratefully accepted China as an ally, after the war they allowed Japan to maintain its absolute interest in Manchuria.

The Rise and Struggles of the Nationalist and Communist Parties

The Russians supported the founding of a Chinese Communist Party (CCP), and at its first Congress in Shanghai, in 1921, two of modern China's great leaders were present – Mao Zedong (Mao Tse-tung) and Zhou Enlai (Chou En-lai). But the Russians also supported the Nationalists (KMT), who were being reorganised by Sun Yat-sen from his base in Guangzhou (Canton). They persuaded the CCP and KMT reluctantly to cooperate, to try to cause revolution in a country still controlled by the warlords and their 'ragged armies'.

Sun Yat-sen was working for power for the peasant population when he died in 1925. He was succeeded as Nationalist leader by Chiang Kai-shek. The CCP was also busily enrolling millions of peasants as members of local associations. These parties had different aims; but, in 1926, each formed an army and marched north from the KMT-controlled southern provinces, under the leadership of Chiang Kai-shek. Agents were sent ahead to organise uprisings. By March 1927, a CCP force had taken Wuhan and the KMT had entered Shanghai – where British troops were sent to guard foreign concessions.

But, suddenly, Chiang Kai-shek's Nationalist forces turned on the CCP and drove the Communists southwards into the eastern hill country. In January 1928, Nanjing (Nanking) was proclaimed capital of the Nationalist Republic of China, and Chiang Kai-shek marched north to take Beijing. During the next few years, ever-increasing numbers of Nationalist troops were used to try to wipe out the Communists. But in 1931 the Japanese invaded Manchuria, and tied up the Nationalist forces. After a Japanese air and naval attack on Shanghai, Chiang Kai-shek agreed to Manchuria becoming an independent state, to be called Manchukuo and ruled by Pu Yi, under the control of Japan.

The Long March

The Nationalists then resumed fighting the Communists. In 1935 they forced some 100 000 from their settlements in an isolated hilly part of Jiangxi province. Under Mao Zedong, this *Red Army* fought its way westwards across China and into the mountains bordering Tibet. Turning north, they crossed the Chang jiang (Yangtze kiang) and, by the heroic capture of a suspension bridge over a narrow gorge also crossed the torrential waters of the Dadu (Tatu) river. Despite great casualties, they struggled on through snow-covered mountains and down into the open swampy grassland country of the north. They reached Yanan (Yenan) in Shaanxi province after 368 days. There, in the loess lands, the 20 000 survivors settled into hillside caves, in a region which became the heart of Communist development. To the Chinese people, the Long March is an epic story of courage, which allowed their Communist Party to survive.

War Brings a Fragile United Front

Meanwhile, the Nationalists set about seeking help from the world's industrialised countries to provide factories, armaments and better communications, for Japan had taken the iron ores, coal, and heavy industries of the north-east. The Nanjing government also began to make considerable improvements in the richer rural parts of the Chang jiang valley; though huge loans would have been needed to improve conditions for the mass of people outside these areas, and the government lacked support in many regions.

The Japanese, who were watching China begin to build up with outside help, were poised to attack. Mao, who was organising a communist society about Yanan, had already declared war on Japan. He knew that the Chinese must act together in the face of such a powerful enemy. In 1936, pro-communist troops captured Chiang Kai-shek near Xian. He was released after agreeing with the Communist leaders to unite with them in the face of danger; and when, in July 1937, Japan invaded China, the Communists and Nationalists formed a United Front.

The Russians sent aircraft and pilots to help China, and supplies came from the Western nations and America, who had, diplomatically, to

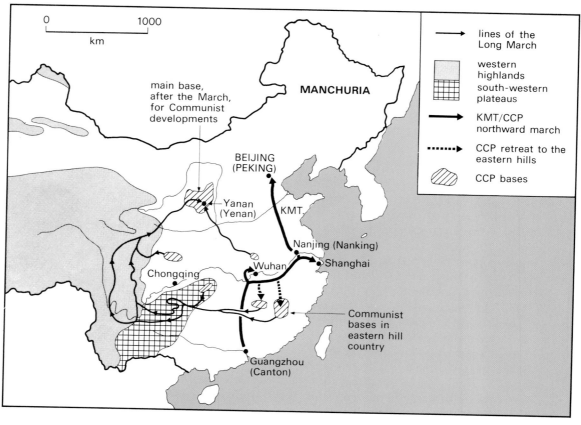

44 *Three military movements which sowed the seeds for the consolidation of Communist activities and the eventual establishment of the People's Republic.*

regard this war as an 'incident'. The Chinese resisted fiercely, but were forced to abandon control of Shanghai, then Nanjing, and then Wuhan, and finally moved their capital far to the west, to Chongqing (Chungking). The Japanese controlled the area shown in Fig. 45, though there was guerilla warfare within this territory, and fighting flared up in other areas. Generally, however, they were content, in view of China's help from other nations, to hold the large cities and the richest lands.

During the Second World War China's supply situation became critical, for the Russians needed their own armaments, and the Japanese invasion of Burma cut the supply route to Chongqing from the south, along the 'Burma Road'. Later, the Americans developed air bases in western China and supplies were flown in from north-east India.

The Japanese were also occupied, of course, with fighting in the Pacific and south-east Asia.

In the meantime, the United Front had little meaning. The Communists in the north were carrying out large-scale guerilla actions against the Japanese; but they were continuing to organise in the north-west a peasant society which accepted reforms along communist principles. While many of the Nationalists in Chongqing regarded World War II as an interruption in their own war against the Communists.

Victory for the People's Liberation Army

When, in 1945, the atomic bomb brought war with Japan to a sudden end, the Communists received large quantities of arms and ammunition from the surrendering Japanese. They made for the vital industrial centres in Manchuria, where the Russians had recently moved in against the Japanese. The Nationalists also rushed northwards; and soon civil war had begun again.

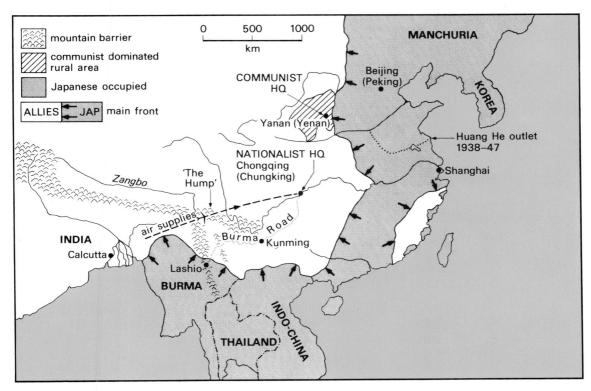

45 *The so-called 'Common Front' jointly resisted the Japanese. It was directed by Chang Kai-shek from the Nationalist capital, Chongqing, but with Mao Zedong firmly controlling Communist activities from Yanan.*

After a series of truces, an all-out civil war began in 1947, and ended only with the general advance, during 1949, of the Chinese Red Army, renamed the People's Liberation Army (PLA). As the PLA advanced, the Chinese Communist Party (CCP) immediately introduced land reforms in the occupied areas, and so won the support of the peasant population. A reputation for absolute honesty surrounded Mao and his close followers, and the people undoubtedly contrasted this with what had gone before. The Nationalist defeat had been hastened by corruption in their midst, and by inflation, which ruined many of their business supporters in the cities.

In October 1949, Mao Zedong, as Chairman of the Chinese Communist Party, announced the creation of the People's Republic of China (PRC), with the government once more located in Beijing. The Nationalist forces were still retreating in the south, and Chiang Kai-shek moved to Taibei

(Taipei), capital of Taiwan, which had been liberated from the Japanese in 1945. Early in 1950, the last of his main forces left Hainan island for Taiwan, to become part of what was widely known as 'Nationalist China', but, in fact, retained the name of the Republic of China (p. 160).

The People's Republic of China (PRC)

The Chinese Communist Party now had to prove to the people that, if they worked together, all might reach a standard of living which had been impossible under centuries of exploitation. They faced great difficulties, for four-fifths of the population could neither read nor write, and the country was ill-organised, shattered by so many years of fighting. Foreigners had relinquished Chinese territory – except for the British in Hong Kong and the Portuguese in Macao. But this had its drawbacks, for most foreign firms and banks had withdrawn and their governments were suspicious of the new regime: the USA did not even recognise the People's Republic, and was backing the government in Taiwan. Rebuilding

46 *The chattering children in Tiananmen square in central Beijing hints at the progress in recent decades, but not at the confrontations of 1989, which cast a dark shadow over their future.*

and developing would be an enormous task.

Most of the population still worked on the land, so that the first move towards gaining the people's confidence was to establish a programme of land reform. Local communist committees were set up all over China to remove the landlords and divide their land among the peasant farmers. There was much violence at first; but many of the former landlords remained to work their share of the land like the other local people, most of whom were cultivating their own small holdings for the first time. In fact, this rearrangement did not greatly help the country's agricultural output; for uneducated farmers working on small plots was not the most efficient way of increasing production. Nevertheless, the first thing was to gain people's confidence, and, despite the upheavals, that had gradually been achieved.

Policies for a Developing Country: What to Tackle First?

The government had to try to find the right balance between agricultural and industrial development. They needed loans to buy equipment to rebuild the country: but loans have to be paid back. Most of the country's trading income came from exporting rural produce, agricultural manufactures and the products of light industries. Hence agriculture had to be made as productive as possible, not only to feed the people, but to grow produce for export, and also to encourage rural industries.

At the same time, China needed heavy industries to produce iron and steel and other metals, and to make the machinery required for building new railways, trucks, aircraft, dams and armaments. Factories had to be set up to manufacture the agricultural implements and everyday goods required by the people. Men and women, who now had equal rights, needed special technical training to be able to manage industries and work with new equipment. To undertake all

There were enormous reserves of energy to be developed from the known deposits of coal, oil and gas, and from the rivers. There was a need for better ports and communications. Decisions also had to be made as where best to site new light industries, and how to employ the millions of city dwellers, to enable them to make their best contribution to the state.

Side by side with all this there had to be great efforts to improve the education, health and welfare of the people, and to keep the population growth under control. Population control is now seen as an absolute priority, for the 600 million in 1949 has grown to more than a thousand million, putting pressure on all the country's resources.

From the 'Fifties to the 'Eighties: An Outline of Events

During the nineteen-fifties, the Russians continued to help the Chinese build up their heavy industries and increase the output of coal and electricity. But in the countryside production still lagged. Farming in general needed more machinery, more fertilisers, more electricity and better transport; and the government looked for a system of cultivation which would lead to higher productivity. If the agricultural output could be improved, there would be a better market for rural industries and not just those which produced the much needed chemicals and farm machinery. For instance, extra income from farming could also be used to develop local processing factories.

At first the peasants were encouraged to form teams and cultivate their family lands by sharing their labour, animals and implements. Next, voluntary cooperatives were set up, in which groups of people cooperated by pooling their land. They marketed their produce centrally, and distributed the income among themselves according to the land provided and the work done by each member. Larger cooperatives were then formed, so that whole villages could take part, and thus have more capital to buy machinery and establish rural industries. The income was again distributed to each member according to the work he or she had done. Local governments helped these 'advanced cooperatives': but the Party (CCP) leaders, directed by Mao Zedong, felt that the *whole* way of life of the countryside should be

this, energy sources had to be developed, and, of course, that, too, called for much new and expensive equipment: though, wherever possible, man-power was used in large construction projects, such as dam building.

The Chinese leaders had to decide what should be given top priority for development, and to ensure that one sector did not lag behind the others. In 1950, China signed a Treaty of Friendship and Alliance with the USSR. This was very important to China, for the Russians provided loans, supplied equipment and technicians, and helped to train skilled workers. This enabled China to build new heavy industries in the damaged cities of the north-east (Manchuria), and in other industrial cities, such as Wuhan (p. 110). Their factories began to produce parts needed for engineering, agricultural machinery, coal mines and oil plant, and to manufacture military equipment, for China could not relax its defences; and, indeed, the PLA was soon engaged in North Korea, in the war of 1950–53.

re-organised as far as possible, and made new proposals.

In 1958, Mao Zedong announced new plans which were designed to bring about a 'Great Leap Forward'. People's Communes were set up to create rural development over large areas. They were not simply to manage agriculture, but to help with local administration, organise social and political life, and build up light rural industries. They were to be responsible for fairly large schemes, such as providing irrigation canals and water storages. Private ownership of land was ended. In this year, over half a million cooperatives were merged into tens of thousands of communes. There were regional variations, but for many years the communes formed the basis of rural life in most parts of China (p. 51).

Other parts of the Great Leap Forward were less successful, particularly the attempt to spread industrial production over the whole country. Iron and steel were to be produced in small furnaces set up wherever possible, and manufacturing industries were to be widely distributed, to bring about rapid industrialisation. This proved a mistake; and unfortunately, two other upsets occurred at the same time. China and

47 An agricultural development scheme, organised by a commune which established the tree belt to the left, shows the value of man-power for large projects. Notice the efficient use of simple well-constructed carts.

the USSR quarrelled over the direction their communist policies were going. The USSR withdrew all aid and technicians, leaving China's future progress almost entirely in its own hands. Then climatic conditions brought a series of disastrous harvests in various parts of the country.

In 1961, the Great Leap Forward was abandoned. Nevertheless, the communes had proved generally successful, and the right to hold small private plots was then restored to the families. Increasing rural productivity began to encourage small-scale industries to be set up away from the large centres of population. Chemical and fertiliser factories and processing plants were established in the rural areas.

China, without imports from the USSR, now had to mass-produce such things as tractors and aircraft in its own factories, and continue with its nuclear energy programme on its own. Only absolute essentials were brought from other

nations, with earnings from export of coal and agricultural produce. It was now a policy of self-reliance; but progress did continue.

But as China's industries grew, some Communist Party leaders saw that this might lead to a new privileged class of scientists, engineers, managers and so on; and this was against their communist principles. They also saw that as foreign methods were adopted, Western ways of thinking might influence the people. Because of this, in 1966, Mao Zedong began a campaign, known as the Cultural Revolution. He formed millions of young people into *Red Guards*, to take action against those who had showed 'bourgeois beliefs'. Many liberal thinkers, politicians, scientists, teachers and students were imprisoned, or sent to do agricultural work on communes in various parts of the country. Minority peoples and religious groups also suffered. Monasteries, mosques and churches were closed. There was much violence throughout China, and actions against foreigners and foreign influences which unfortunately cut off contacts which might have helped China in its plan to modernise. There was depression and near-starvation in some rural areas, and distrust of the Party among peasants in

48 Immense investment was needed to build this 1100 km line from Kunming, through the mountains, to Chengdu – the train is inside tunnels for 500 km in all, and there are numerous bridges. The train crosses a deep ravine, and even here are ricefields, with heaps of manure and seedlings growing. It highlights China's priority problems: which to develop first – heavy industry, engineering, transportation, agriculture, social organisation? Each depends on the other.

various parts of the country. Things became so chaotic in some regions that the PLA had to be called to restore order. Eventually the Red Guards were disbanded. Yet Mao remained in control, for his past achievements and his broad ideals were respected by the mass of the people.

During the 'seventies, especially after American withdrawal from Vietnam, there were more direct contacts with the USA, Japan and European countries. At long last, in 1971, the People's Republic was admitted as a member of the United Nations, and Taiwan displaced. Yet the USA did not fully recognise the PRC until 1979.

When Mao Zedong died, in 1976, changes began to take place within the Communist Party. A struggle for power led to the arrest and trial of

Mao's widow and her associates, known as the 'Gang of Four', and to control by men with an outlook favouring modernisation and more contacts with the West. They created new trade links and sought industrial help from other countries. Foreign firms were licensed to operate in parts of China and form joint manufacturing ventures, though not to own land.

Individual families and collective groups now engage in private businesses, or contract to use land for specific purposes, and sell excess produce on the open market. This has brought rewards for initiative and skill, and given many families greater purchasing power. Though this is low compared with people in First World countries, there has been immense progress away from the backwardness and poverty of the 1940s.

However, the market economy system has brought problems of inflation and opportunities for corruption. There is also frustration among those who look for more liberal policies and greater democracy in the hierarchical structure of government.

The communist-dominated government has sought to maintain rigid centralised control over the vast population and, if necessary, to back its decisions with military action. In 1989 protests against alleged corruption and restrictions of democratic processes, voiced mainly by students, led to responses which have affected China's international relationships, and may have repercussions for industrial joint-venture developments.

Points to Consider

1 During China's long history it absorbed different invading peoples, whose rulers adopted many of its traditional customs.
2 The power of the early states and influences of later invasions made northern China the dominant part of the country. Consolidation and expansion under the Han dynasty led to the greater population being known as the 'Han Chinese'.
3 Confucianism, Daoism, and Buddhism were accepted at various times, and a blend of their ideas has influenced the patterns of behaviour of rulers, officials, and subjects alike.
4 The continuation of China's dynastic rule, with strict observance of traditions and inward-looking policies, resulted in great contrasts between China and European nations during the 18th and 19th centuries.
5 European interference led to many deplorable incidents; but the development of Treaty settlements, and the resulting commerce, forced China into greater contacts with the West.
6 The 19th century Taiping rebellion first demonstrated peasant power.

7 Civil wars in the early days of the Republic held China back; but the Long March, and the behaviour of the PLA during the advances of 1948–49, were milestones in winning over the mass of the people to communism.
8 The agricultural reorganisation in the 1950s brought enthusiastic response and rapid results from the rural population. But difficulties in balancing heavy industrial and agricultural progress persisted through the 1960s.
9 The benefits under communism were initially a spur to future progress. But 'extreme left' policies of equality in all things, during the Cultural Revolution, put a brake on development and caused near-disaster in many fields.
10 A more liberal approach, with incentives and rewards from a restricted market economy, has created economic development, with rapid social changes; though the state exercises firm central controls.
11 Citizens, students especially, seeking to broaden narrow central control, have triggered horrific counter-actions, with potentially serious international responses.

49 *Heavy-leaved lotus and taro plants grown as root crops in the humid lowlands of south-east Guangdong.*

3 Modern China: Rural Activities in Different Areas

The State Control over Rural Activities

The provinces of China are shown on page x. Among China's thousand million people are some eighty million non-Han Chinese. Parts of the country are known as *Autonomous Regions* (AR), in which national minority groups have partial self-government. There are also smaller areas within provinces and ARs where other minority groups have some control over their own affairs. Besides the provinces and ARs, the state also directly administers three great city areas (municipalities): Beijing (Peking), Tianjin (Tientsin), and Shanghai.

Within the provinces there are smaller units, through which China's large population can be administered as efficiently as possible (Fig. 50).

A *province* directly administers a number of *prefectures* and large cities, which are usually well developed industrially. Each prefecture looks after its group of *county* units and cities. Each county has numerous market towns, usually with small factories making light products for local consumption.

Various townships act as administrative centres for villages and other rural communities in the countryside about them. The elected township head and committee members are links between officials at the county town and cadres elected by the local rural population. They decide on land allocation to those contracting responsibility for its use, and are concerned with rural production, local industries, commerce and trade. They also deal with education, welfare and public health, civil administration, and local works, and with the extent of local funding of these. They now have much closer contacts with the individuals, families, and collective groups engaged on contract work, for this has increased movements between homes and townships; though, in general, rural people remain part of their local village (brigade) even when closely engaged in retailing or industrial activities in the local town. Communist Party representatives on committees help to ensure that official policies are carried out in each aspect of rural life; though in recent years local flexibility has been advocated.

50 The chain of control through which this huge country is administered and by means of which production can be organised by the state. Today township committees arrange responsibility contracts for production, and experts from provincial and county specialist units pass down advice on technology at grass roots level.

Rural China: Organisation

China is still essentially a rural country. Its surplus agricultural products create most of the capital used for the country's development. Hence agriculture must strive both to support a

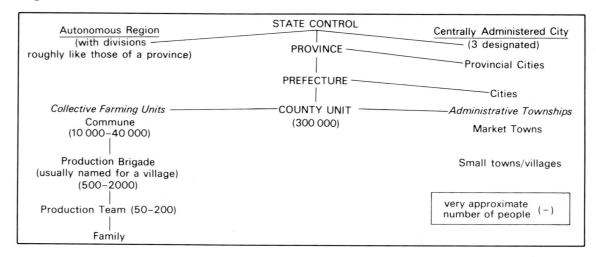

51 Villagers at Xiobanqiao bundling rice seedlings for transplanting in their flooded fields. The collective group contracts to be responsible for production from land allotted about the village.

population which increases by more than ten million a year and to provide raw materials for the country's industries, and for export.

Much of the land which can be cultivated has already been farmed for a long time: so that any increase in agricultural production must largely depend on providing more efficient mechanical aids, more fertilisers and pesticides, or improved varieties of seeds; and on introducing methods which will obtain a higher yield from existing land. In so large a country this requires a careful distribution of state resources and efficient organisation of the rural population: for in the end improvements in rural production depend largely on the achievements of families and individuals.

The prosperity of rural communities varies with location. In some parts of the country the rural population struggles to obtain a reasonable increase in living standards. Those living near the larger cities have great advantages in obtaining equipment, and in their marketing opportunities; and, being richer, have better social amenities. But though others are less fortunate, these more prosperous communities represent the standards which the state is trying to establish throughout the country, provide 'targets' for others to aim at, and create wealth which can ultimately benefit the whole population.

Some parts of China which have remained sparsely inhabited, through persistent droughts, floods, or unfavourable climatic conditions have been reclaimed and turned into large state farms. This has been done by providing machinery on a large scale, for land reclamation and for use in the actual farming. Millions of people have been settled in this way in the marginal areas, especially in the north-east, where winters are cold and long, in the dry lands of the interior, and in difficult hill country in the south.

Why the Role of the Communes Changed

Within each county communes were broadly responsible for the farming activities of the tens of thousands, or sometimes hundreds of

52 Wooded countryside with broad-leaf trees and bamboos to the west of the Sichuan basin, where parcels of land about a village have been allocated to families who contract to cultivate it. The family group has separate strips of land, some good, some less good. In many villages the responsibility system has led to the formation of collective groups who arrange to pool land and, where possible, to create continuous areas which can be farmed more efficiently with the help of simple machinery. Individuals may then be freed to concentrate on sideline activities, which in this area include forestry, timber milling, and making furniture and fencing.

thousands, of people who lived under their administration. Their elected management committee arranged with the State Planning Organisation the targets for what they would produce during the year. They decided how best to use the land in their particular part of the country, and discussed their proposals with their brigades, whose elected officials organised daily tasks for their production teams. They also organised such practical things as water control, tree planting, road improvements and seasonal repair works. They established rural industries and organised work in local factories.

A commune was required annually to produce a certain quantity of a particular commodity (a quota); and so it established quotas for the various brigades and teams. The state fixed the price to be paid for such commodities as grain, oilseeds, and cotton, for that year.
The brigade committees supervised local production of grain, cash crops, vegetables, and

livestock through the production teams. Unfortunately the system was apt to be operated in defiance of local conditions. As quotas were fixed at provincial and county levels, grain-growing tended to be emphasised, often at the expense of what might locally prove to be a more suitable and profitable cash crop.

A production team might comprise 20–30 families from a village, or from more scattered homesteads. A leader was elected, periodically, to organise the daily tasks. Individuals were expected to work a six-day week. They received wages, based on profits from the quota sold to the state and any surplus marketed locally, in proportion to the work put in; though a basic minimum was guaranteed.

A portion of the village land was divided among the families; each of whom had a small area on which to grow vegetables, fruit, or fodder, and keep chickens or pigs. They might thus consume part of the produce and sell the rest in a local market, bringing a welcome addition to the family income.

For a long time the communes also organised processing industries, the maintenance of machinery and draught animals, and service occupations. They looked after education, political activities, health and welfare. This general organisation ensured that, barring climatic disasters, people were able to live above the bare subsistence level; and those in favoured locations might enjoy a higher standard of living. Yet, overall, the commune system led to stagnation and failure to develop the full potential of the land. There was little incentive for teams or individuals to use initiative in an egalitarian society which gave little extra award for effort, while guaranteeing a basic standard of living.

On the positive side, communes could be organised to undertake large projects, such as road building, canal construction, or major industrial development, with payment through the normal brigade structure. Communes from adjoining counties could easily be combined to work on extensive schemes. The People's Liberation Army (PLA) with its specialist construction groups is also involved with peaceful construction projects (which makes its hard-line role in suppressing civil demonstrations such a contrast).

Nevertheless the generally low productivity under the commune system was failing to meet the needs of the growing population in a nation aiming at economic development. The same applied to the state-controlled industries, where factories often carried an excess labour force, and workers were assured of a job and basic rations – their 'iron rice bowl'. There were few incentives for extra effort or for initiative by management, which had little control over materials, marketing, or investment of profits.

As a result, major policy changes altered the role of the communes and introduced new practices in manufacturing industries. In the countryside an appointed township became the basic unit of local government. For those living in villages and rural homesteads, the commune's role in organising a chain of collective production units was replaced by the introduction of the contract responsibility system. Village cadres no longer organise tasks for rural communities operating as teams, but liaise with the elected township head and officials about the practicalities of land distribution and necessary communal work, such as canal maintenance and road improvements; though the latter is less easy to arrange now that individuals are concentrating on their private occupations. Township officials register land allotments and small enterprises undertaken by individuals, families, or collective groups, and collect taxes and dues for welfare purposes.

53 *A few of the millions of young trees planted in the loess lands form an avenue leading to a village. The carts used by the teams have well maintained wheels and bearings and are easy to pull. Winter winds are very cold here – notice the thick garments.*

The Collective Responsibility System

It is now the practice for individuals or groups to sign a contract to provide a certain amount of produce from land allocated to them – though not owned by them – and to sell this contracted quota to the state at agreed prices. They may then sell extra produce on the open market should they wish to do so. The state may wish to offer more for extra produce, and to maintain this offer should market prices fall below this level.

Once the system was introduced, with such incentives, productivity increased dramatically. People now wish to improve their methods of production and produce as much as possible. Contracts can also be made in respect of other rural activities, such as fishing, forestry, or brick-making; or to set up a small manufacturing unit; or to retail goods for profit, and so contribute to the state through taxes. Rural families with an allocation of land to cultivate often take up other sideline activities. As a result, family incomes have been increasing considerably, especially in the well-favoured regions. They pay tax on their income and contribute to the local administrative

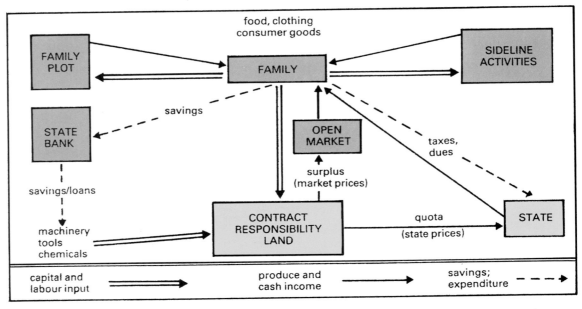

54 *Distribution of produce, income, and investment for a family contracting with a township committee under the Responsibility System.*

offices for welfare and other services.

It pays people to invest in simple machinery and improve forms of intermediate technology. County-administered specialist training groups find that people are now very responsive to new methods and new forms of machinery, and to new ways of tackling perennial problems such as crop diseases, pest damage, soil erosion, and so on. This applies particularly to small specialist contract groups engaging in duck farming, fish raising, forestry, or tractor maintenance, with earnings linked to their output or results.

In some respects the freedom from rigid controls worked against the wishes of the central administration. In some areas, for instance, grain production has fallen below the desired amount, as people have turned from wheat- or rice-growing, at least on some of their land, and engaged in vegetable-growing, fruit farming, or producing a profitable crop likely to bring in a higher income than grain. This has necessitated upward adjustment of rewards to the farmers for grain production, and so made grain more expensive for urban consumers. There have been state subsidies to keep prices down in urban markets, but the situation is one cause of urban unrest.

Under this system most families live in the same rural communities and cultivate land about the village or homestead; and though the nature of the cultivation, their livestock, and the structure of the settlements themselves vary from region to region, the economic pattern of their activities will be along the lines summarised in Fig. 54. But the ability of families to save and re-invest varies considerably, especially between settlements well-located in relation to markets and those in more remote areas.

Savings in state banks are now encouraged and loans are made available where appropriate, for they may be used to increase production through the purchase of tools and machinery, fertilisers or pesticides, or to help with the consolidation of holdings. In some of the richer counties in eastern China successful individuals or collectives have arranged for large amounts of land to be allocated for their mangement, with specialists and labourers working for wages.

The extent to which individuals can obtain entitlement to land is still not clear. The present trend is a far cry from the land distribution arrangements under the commune system, and a political debating point within China. Such radical changes over such a short period of time are bound to necessitate policy adjustments; for efficient rural production, rewarded by increasing opportunities, can go hand in hand with local speculation and unfair profiteering, which require government controls.

The Value of Intermediate Technology

Practical advice from county agricultural experts is usually simple but effective, Chinese farmers learn to make efficient use of available machinery and materials. Machinery which needs a lot of fuel to run it may be uneconomic. It is often better to use 'intermediate technology' which makes the best of human energy through simple machinery. The handcart is widely used throughout China, both on the farms and in construction work. Its use may suggest hard labour and rural poverty; but these carts usually have serviceable tyres and efficient axles and bearings and may easily be pulled when laden, thus making the most of the available energy. Horses and carts are also widely employed and usually equally efficient. Nevertheless, small power units and tractors are being increasingly used on the land and for local transport, and many are now manufactured regionally.

The intensive cultivation of vegetables is a feature of rural, and even urban, life in China. Chemical fertilisers, humus, alluvium from ditch clearance, and night soil and refuse from houses, treated, and in some cases made into small briquettes, are all used to increase productivity. A recent directive to village communities in Yunnan stressed the importance of widening the raised earth ridges bounding the fields, so that beans might be grown on them. Most of the people are conscious of, and enthusiastic about improvements at their local level, and acknowledge the value of careful organisation.

Daily Life in Rural Communities

Conditions vary considerably in different parts of the country. So do opportunities opened up by the contract system. Yet there are common patterns in the life of rural people.

Families usually obtain a loan to buy their house, so no rent is required. Parents may help newly-weds buy building materials, and contract builders may construct a house. Many people are building new homes; but expanding villages take up agricultural land, so building is being restricted to poor quality sites.

Basic education is free, though small contributions may be made for meals or books. Nursery schools may allow mothers to add to the family income: otherwise elderly relatives look after the young. Boys and girls then go to primary schools, junior middle schools, and, if qualified, to senior schools for secondary education, perhaps in another part of the county. The

55 Sources of income for a rural family in Hunan.

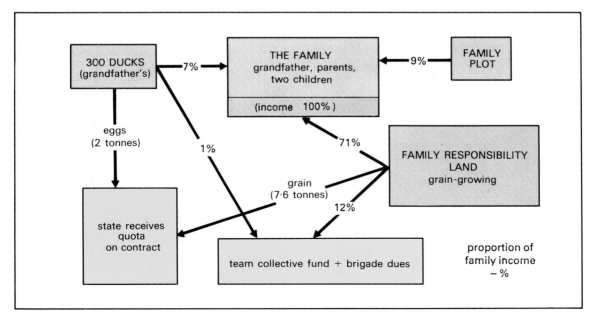

56 A locally made wheat winnowing machine in a large village west of Chengdu.

education is general, but practical. It encourages skilled technical work for local use. There is also political education. Nearly every child becomes a Young Pioneer and wears a red neckerchief when they meet together.

Standards of education vary with location and availability of trained teachers. Most young people in peasant families, however, find it difficult to pass exams for secondary schools, and few go on to higher education. There is a shortage of places at higher technical institutes and universities, and thus tremendous competition. Time spent on farm work in busy seasons, and lower standards of rural teaching make it difficult for them to compete with their urban counterparts.

The army has offered opportunities for peasant youths, and there was great demand to serve in the PLA; but with a streamlined standing army only a small proportion could be accepted. Most, therefore, remain in the rural district.

Committees in the small towns arrange welfare work and various free local services, which usually include running water. There are services for which people pay small amounts, or contribute to welfare funds. A number of local

people are trained as paramedics, able to decide what is wrong with patients and give simple treatment; they learn to pass on the seriously ill to regional hospitals; they also look after, and give advice on, hygiene, health and family planning. Welfare funds are also used to take care of people handicapped by accident, sickness or old age; though, in general, old people remain part of the family home.

In the richer areas such as those near the cities, township committees organise social centres with a library, radios and TV sets. Most families have a radio and may save to buy a TV for the home. There is much enthusiasm for recreational activities, and various kinds of gymnastics, basket ball, table tennis and football are universally popular. Keeping fit takes many forms, and is usually on a personal basis, with special exercises for the old; it is a visible part of life in city and country alike, where people singly, or in groups, carry out the slow balanced movements of Tai Ji Quan (Tai Chi Chuan). In some parts of the countryside living standards are much lower, but there are usually rooms in the villages for public use, spaces set aside for recreation, and public bathhouses in the small towns.

57 Girls sort cocoons at a collectively owned silk factory near Jing Ma on the Chengdu plains.

58 Pigs have been pushed in from surrounding villages to a factory near Langshan in the loess lands.

59 A free market in Jinghong, on the Lancang jiang (Mekong river), where Dai women are selling vegetables.

Traditional markets held periodically in streets in small towns offer excess rural produce and many goods made locally – baskets, pipes, brooms, spades, hinges and other small metal products. But in most townships people can now buy a wide range of consumer goods at cooperative stores and small shops in the market towns and villages, or from the booths of licensed street traders. There is now a variety of attractive materials for women and children, though men dress less colourfully. In the north cheap, tough blue working overalls, jackets and trousers, and the padded jackets are practical garments for everyday wear during winter. Colour is certainly not lacking in the minority areas, where the people often wear colourful traditional clothing (Fig. 59).

Most people save for a bicycle, and millions of sturdy machines, produced by Chinese factories, are ridden to and from work and between village and town. Other things that all families buy are crockery and vacuum flasks. Water is boiled, for safety, and in every household, and at refreshment stalls along the streets, there are large flasks filled with drinking water, or ready for tea-making.

Besides these things, the stores stock watches, sewing machines, transistors, toilet products, toothpaste, a range of household goods and

decorations, toys, bunting and fireworks for celebrations, condiments and sweets and so on. Ironmongers have the usual variety of practical products for home and garden. Competition now helps to control prices, though the government guides price limits. In a country as large as China the cost of transport causes regional variations.

In the homes, the cost of supplying energy for heating, cooking and lighting can be kept down in a number of ways. People used to the conservation of resources have taken readily to burning methane gas, produced from household and farm waste in the kind of apparatus described on p. 99. This is used in addition to the electricity which is now supplied to most settlements, often from small, local generating plants.

The State Farms

In order to develop marginal farmland and increase production from large areas of under-used land, the government set up *state farms*, which were not part of the county township organisation. In most cases the state provided the expensive machinery needed to reclaim the waste land, construct drainage and irrigation canals,

60 *A village of some two hundred people near Langshan in the loess lands. Compare this nucleated settlement and its buildings with those in Fig. 61 Notice the shuttering marks on the walls: see Fig. 5.*

61 *Settlement on the Chengdu plains, where family houses are clustered in groups amid trees and clumps of bamboo. The small factory to the left processes rape seed from the crop grown in the fields now flooded for rice.*

prepare the soil for farming, and create settlements. Machinery was generally supplied for seeding, harvesting and other activities; for, with large farms, this is usually a form of extensive cultivation.

Many of the state farms are in the north-east, where the rich steppe soils invite cultivation but the long, severe winters make settlement unattractive for peasant farming. With direct state control of machinery and labour, a large amount of land could be made productive as quickly and efficiently as possible. Many of the families settled on the state farms have come from areas where over-population led to much rural poverty, in parts of Shandong, for example (p. 64). Life was particularly hard here during the pioneer stages of development. But when established, the family life on the farms since the introduction of the responsibility system, is not unlike that in other village communities. When work on the land is restricted by winter cold, people are employed on construction projects, repairing machinery, maintaining canals and other projects.

State farms have been established in the dry interior of Xinjiang, where intricate water-supply systems need overall control, and pioneer farming calls for careful supervision. Many Han Chinese transferred here from the east; large numbers came from the cities, especially during the time of the Cultural Revolution.

In the hilly country of south-eastern China, families with little experience of farming have been directed to state farms for training and settlement; not only those from the cities, but Chinese returned from abroad, many of them refugees. There are also state farms in the south-western highlands, where shifting cultivation has been discouraged and the pattern of farming is being reorganised.

The government encourages the establishment of *demonstration farms*. These are mainly run by the counties, with state aid, which enables them to experiment with methods of increasing production suited to their own locality. The results, are demonstrated to suitable people selected from the villages, who are thus encouraged to introduce better ways of cultivation or raising stock.

Points to Consider

1 The chain of authority (Fig. 50) with its political advisers at all levels makes it possible for government decisions to be passed to rural cadres and families, the foundation of this huge, closely controlled population.
2 A vast bureaucracy like this has disadvantages. The central policies may not suit local conditions. Also, with so many officials to consult and views to be heard, necessary reforms can be hindered.
3 The system works well when the people really do have a say in their own affairs; and the introduction of the responsibility system greatly increased productivity.
4 China's social advances are concerned with the activities and welfare of a vast rural population. For some, labour-saving machinery may mean under-employment: intermediate technology may be preferable to more advanced forms.
5 More efficient rural production produces more wealth for the families, and leads to demands for products from workshops and factories; which give more local employment.
6 A difficult problem is the inequality of opportunities for those in well-favoured locations and those in poorer, often remote, regions.
7 The 'responsibility system' has increased productivity, but has created greater differences in income. There is debate as to how it matches communist principles.
8 Under the responsibility system a larger family may have advantages; this tends to act against the 'one-child family' campaign.
9 Lack of opportunity for higher education in rural areas, and difficulties of employment in towns, means that many young people remain in the countryside, close to where they were born. There are advantages and disadvantages in this.

Rural Activities in Different Parts of China

Northern China

The Dazhai Example: Its Limitations

The hillsides of the north make a good starting place, for here, in 1953, in an eroded, gullied landscape, the local people began to organise their communal activities in a manner which was later held up as an example to the rest of China. At Dazhai (Tachai) families combined their holdings in order to make large-scale improvements through their own efforts. Together they terraced the broken hillsides for wheat-growing, dug carefully contoured systems of irrigation ditches, and planted fruit trees. Later, as the Dazhai brigade of the local commune, their productivity was said to be so great that Mao Zedong encouraged progress elsewhere with the phrase 'In agriculture, learn from Dazhai'. The people, well-organised, had undoubtedly worked hard; but their later production figures, issued for propaganda purposes, have since been queried;

and, in practice, the policy of trying to apply what had happened at Dazhai to other parts of China proved a mixed blessing. In many cases it interfered with other methods better suited to the local conditions – an illustration of the dangers of central propaganda and the insistence on strictly conforming with regulations. Today, there are moves towards greater regional freedom. Nevertheless, the efforts at Dazhai are typical of the energy put into making the most of unfavourable conditions, and show how great was the response of so many peasant people to the land reorganisation which followed the creation of the People's Republic.

The Loess Lands

In the loess lands the people have long terraced hillsides as an effective means of providing level stretches for cultivation and partly controlling erosion. But even the older terraced lands had become seriously gullied; so that the more recent methods of improving the productivity of the loess lands combine terracing with other ways of

62 The northern hill country and plains which drain to the Huang He and Gulf of Bohai.

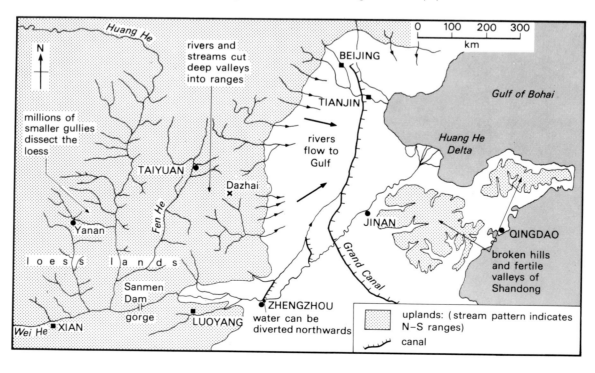

preventing soil loss, delivering water and controlling run-off from the surface.

Today, most of the contours in the loess lands are followed by wide, sweeping terraces. Earthen dams are built across many of the gullies, so that materials washed down the slopes accumulate behind them, and eventually form a surface which can be cultivated. Apart from the local irrigation systems, there are large reservoirs and wide, lined canals built with the help of state funds. Millions of trees, mostly eucalypts, have recently been planted, on the hillsides and in lines across the wider, flatter valleys, so that they help to hold soil on the slopes, act as windbreaks, and also provide timber. They extend along banks, line the roads in depth, and enclose villages. Afforestation is a major policy throughout China. Here, in the dry north, it is transforming the landscape; as are the lines of pylons and cables running across the countryside, which reflect the electric power developments (p. 96).

Most of the improvements and increased productivity of the land depend on the work and efficient organisation of the people themselves.

63 Loess slopes, surmounted by the tomb of the Tang empress Wu, are terraced and sown with wheat, like those of the surrounding, dissected countryside. A steep-sided erosion channel runs from left to right. Pits can be seen which contain sheltered houses and storerooms (Fig. 65).

The communes provide pumps to deliver water to Electric pumps now deliver water to channels in the dry fields. Farm machinery is widely used. Mini-tractors run along the tree-lined roads between villages; their trailers carry people and produce into the local town, where workshops maintain the vehicles and machinery used by the local teams. Yet well-organised labour is still the key asset. Lines of people cultivating the fields still use China's universal implement, the hoe, to great effect; horses and oxen still pull ploughs and harrows; and alongside the fields rows of handcarts, tipped ready for use, are a common sight — and are often attached to bicycles.

Local mechanisation now tends to be financed by contracting collective groups of villagers from their own savings. Loans for this purpose can be

64 A small settlement in Shanxi in a valley cut into thick, heavily eroded loess; in winter, with fields bare and dry and a trickle of water frozen in the river bed.

arranged, at a small rate of interest, through a local branch of the Chinese People's State Bank. Some building and electrical installations are local village responsibilities, though contracted specialists may go from village to village, as needed.

Here in the north, bricks are used for building, and clay pits and small kilns for brick-making are common features near the towns and villages. However, most of the walls of the terraces, compounds and some of the houses are built in the traditional way, by tamping earth firmly between horizontal poles arranged to form a vertical shuttering. Loess particles readily adhere to one another. This can be seen on the natural hillsides and in the gullies, where the slopes of the soft material remain surprisingly steep. For this reason, many of the older houses were simply caves in the loess slopes. Inside them, the firm, yellow loess walls were polished and plastered, giving a dry shelter, warm in winter and cool in summer. Today, caves are mostly used as stores

and workrooms; though in hilly land houses are often built in hollows in the loess, sheltered from the bitter winds, and those on the plains are surrounded by compound walls.

The loess lands produce heavy yields of wheat, millet, maize, and cotton as cash crops. Pigs are reared by specialists on contract and also by families. Lines of fat pigs strapped to handcarts can be seen queued up outside small meat factories. Maize stalks chopped into pig manure is a useful fertiliser. The carefully tended personal plots, with their cabbage, onions, beans and spinach benefit from pig and chicken manure and village refuse. But most of it goes to village fields, together with chemical fertiliser, delivered in white sacks from regional factories.

The people work long hours during summer. The variety of cash crops needs continuous attention — irrigation, fertiliser spreading, weeding, harvesting and threshing. Then there are the efforts of producing extra food from the family land. People take few days off until later in the year, when they may have a longer break: although winter is a time for repairing terraces, facing wells, and making local improvements.

The Northern Plains

Moving eastwards across northern China, there are noticeable differences in the landscape. There are now very large fields on the plains of the Huang He and on flats in the tributary valleys. In these closely populated lands, the average size of the fields was once only half a hectare. Today they are often 20 hectares, so that machinery can be used more efficiently. Thousands of small villages, with mud-brick houses, are distributed over the wide landscape, and many of the small market towns are still partly enclosed by walls, often bearing slogans in large white characters. The flat landscape is again broken by tree-lined roads and railways, by electric pylons, and by small factories near the towns.

Work in the fields is more continuous through the year in these eastern parts. Besides the winter wheat and barley, which are usually harvested in June, there are summer crops of soya beans, sweet potatoes, kaoliang, and groundnuts, which are lifted in October. Cotton is also well suited by the dry autumn. Some of the fields, especially those near the wandering watercourses, are enclosed by low banks to allow a summer rice crop. Each year a lot of labour is needed to repair the main river dykes; for, despite the great flood control schemes, summer floods are still a danger. The PLA is often called in to help with such tasks.

Farming near the larger cities is often highly mechanised. A small district of some 25 000 people on the yellow-grey loamy soils of south Beijing may have 30–40 tractors and a number of combines, and is likely to support dairy herds as well as pigs, ducks and chicken — all of which help to supply the urban population. Besides their crops of grain, fodder, cotton and oilseeds, the families also grow fruits and vegetables in quantity for the city market. Energy from the electric grid powers the numerous pumping stations and enables thousands of people to work

65 *The courtyard of a small sheltered house in a pit in the loess, in Shanxi. Storerooms have been cut into the soft, firm rock.*

in light industries — grain milling, factories for feedstuffs and fertilisers, tool manufacturing, and textile production.

Population Pressure in Shandong (Shantung)

These few sections can only give a general impression of life in some of the better farmlands of northern China; but, of course, besides the fertile lands described here, there are many hilly regions in the north which are difficult to farm productively. On the other hand, there are also smaller regions which are productive and closely settled, such as the lowlands in and about the hilly peninsula of Shandong, south of the Huang He delta. The soils of its deforested, eroded uplands are poor; but tens of millions of people are concentrated on the fertile lowland and valley

66 *Fields on a series of low wide terraces on the gently sloping loess west of Xian. Some have spring wheat; others are being prepared for irrigation. Notice the use of oxen and the tractor on the right. Tombs of Tang dignitaries stand above the rural landscape.*

67 *Farmland within the municipality of Beijing, but close to the Yanshan ranges, with wheat interbedded with millet and rows of deciduous fruit trees.*

soils, where the climate is milder than on the northern plains. The region has long been noted for its Shantung silk, from silkworms reared on oakleaves – though production is far less than it was. It is the farmlands, capable of producing high yields of grains, beans, cotton, vegetables and fruits from the valley soils, which have led to great population pressure.

As in other parts of China, the communes campaign to control population by strict family planning; but already large numbers of people have left Shandong for the state farms of the north-east. The tall, large-boned people of Shandong are noted for their ruggedness. They have proved excellent colonists in these harsh regions, where, with the rigors of severe winters, the conditions for pioneer farming have been tough. The same qualities apply to the coastal communities in Shandong, who take their fleets of small boats into the rich fishing grounds of the Yellow Sea and Gulf of Bohai.

The North-East

Fig. 68 (A) shows the steppes of the north-east, where state farms, with their houses, schools, stores, clinics and recreation centres, form a patchwork of settlement on the wide, rolling areas of former grassland. There, with the help of mechanisation, the black earth soils are now farmed for wheat and soya beans.

But within the large state farms and in other parts of the north-east village communities now operate the responsibility system. Here, as in other parts of China, the many big industrial cities receive supplies of grain, meat, vegetables, fruit and milk from the adjoining farmlands. The extremes of climate create problems of supply for these north-eastern cities, as illustrated by conditions at Harbin, in Heilongjiang. Eighty years ago it was just a fishing village on the Songhua (Sungari) river. Now it is an industrial city, with thousands of factories making electrical equipment, turbo-generators, boilers, textiles, chemicals and a host of other products. In summer, there is a flow of fresh rural produce into the city. But in winter, when the temperature can fall to −30°C, milk is sold in frozen bricks or in powdered form, meat can be bought wrapped in dough, frozen and preserved, and late fruits, such as pears, grown locally, are frozen for keeping.

Wasteland on the edge of the city has been converted open, windswept marshy tracts into well-drained, irrigable land. A typical commune to the west of Harbin, with some 30000 people, protected its seventy square kilometres with sufficient trees to form windbreaks stretching, in all, for several thousand kilometres. Fields of wheat and soya beans, fruits and vegetables, support the rural families, whose local processing industries enable them to send noodles, soya products, fresh vegetables and animal produce – pigs, eggs, and powdered milk – to the city markets. Some farmers specialise in chicken farming, others in dairying; and in recent years forms of contract farming have favoured those skilled in a particular occupation. Surface water, now controlled, is channelled into ponds and streams, and stocked with fish. There are similar relationships between rural producers and other city markets in the north-east. Those near Shenyang have built long underground tunnels to act as a winter 'deep-freeze' for their vegetables.

The economically important Daqing oilfield also lies in Heilongjiang province (p. 93). Hundreds of thousands of oilworkers have come to this harsh landscape since the early 1960s, accompanied by farmworker settlers, who now

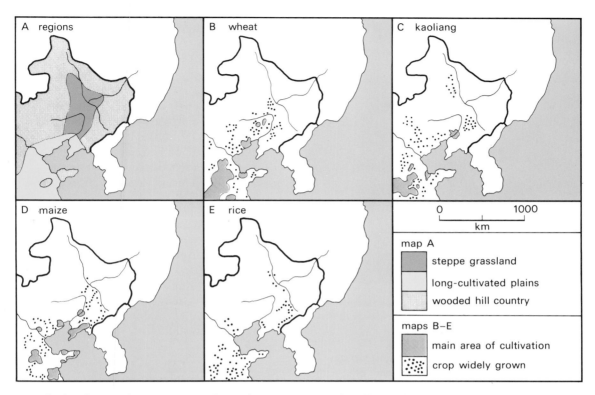

| A regions | B wheat | C kaoliang |
| D maize | E rice | |

map A
- steppe grassland
- long-cultivated plains
- wooded hill country

maps B–E
- main area of cultivation
- crop widely grown

0   1000
km

68 *The distribution of grains grown in the north-east.*

69 *The rolling arable-pastoral countryside of the north-east, with the small houses of an old village amid coniferous and deciduous trees; sunflowers grow in the family gardens.*

Many of the more recent settlements among the forests of the far north-east of Heilongjiang province suffered severely during the forest fires in May 1987, which swept through mountain woodlands along a 250 km wide band. Some 200 people lost their lives and 50 000 were made homeless. PLA units rescued tens of thousands, and military aircraft seeded clouds to produce rain. Nearly a million hectares of valuable timber was destroyed, a serious blow for a country with a shortage of wood and extensive afforestation.

70 The regular pattern of a newer pioneer settlement on flat agricultural land in Heilongjiang province: notice, again, the family vegetable gardens.

contract to cultivate land belonging to villages dispersed over the area about the main oil workings. The immigrant farmers were at first helped by PLA soldiers, many of whom worked on the oilfields in the early days and have stayed to farm the land. Their first mud-brick houses were usually crude, with walls and roofs insulated with layers of mud. Though schools, clinics, stores and canteens have been added, and buildings are more substantial, many of the villages on these open grasslands are still 'frontier-like' settlements, compared with those of the long-established communities further south. But, nevertheless, they produce wheat, maize, soya beans, sorghum, and vegetables, and rear animals on what was looked on as a wasteland before the oil-rush. In the long-run, as oil reserves decline, this will remain as an agriculturally developed marginal region.

But, of course, the north-east is a large and varied part of China. In the milder southern parts there is a much greater variety of crops — groundnuts, sugar beet, cotton, soya beans, tobacco, and fruits, and, in some areas, a summer crop of rice: a striking contrast to the more remote state farms and pasturelands of the far north, and to the small farms about the mining communities in the forested hills of the eastern ranges.

Points to Consider

1 It seems that the Party itself has learned a lesson from the way that all Chinese were encouraged to 'learn from Dazhai'.
2 The physical properties of loess are very important – the way the tiny particles stick together, yet, when loosened, can be carried by the wind; and also its softness and porosity as a rock.
3 Tree-planting is one of China's most important large-scale projects.
4 The activities of villages and state farms vary a great deal across northern China, from the loess lands to the north-east.
5 Climatic factors are partly responsible for the contrasts in the north between some fertile areas with overpopulated farmlands and others with relatively sparse populations.
6 Urban populations greatly influence land-use in the surrounding countryside.
7 Rural activities vary with the season and need careful organisation, even in winter.

Central China

The Middle and Lower Basins of the Chang Jiang (Yangtze Kiang)

The fertile lowland soils of this part of China have been closely cultivated for a very long time. Here is a green, more humid countryside. The surface water of the lakes and flooded fields, and the larger proportion of rice-growing, give these landscapes a different appearance from the plains of the north.

The eye picks up scenes of intensive farming and misty lakes, made familiar by artists over the centuries. Groups of people still engage in the continuous labour needed for rice cultivation — controlling the water, preparing seed beds, transplanting the seedlings, weeding, harvesting and threshing. But now women work side by side with men, and more and more machines are used for ploughing, spraying, reaping, and in some places transplanting the seedlings. There have been experiments with aerial sowing, but with China's great manpower and the amount of fuel this would need, the traditional methods are likely to continue. Nevertheless, small tractors are now part of the rural scenery, as well as the oxen and water buffaloes.

Many of the machines, such as tractors and pumps, are made in cities like Wuhan, Changsha and Shanghai; but thousands of smaller factories now manufacture farm machinery, especially the semi-mechanised farm implements and tools used by the local families. Small chemical works produce some of the fertilisers and insecticides needed to maintain soil fertility and increase crop yields; for the soils have almost continuous use throughout the year.

The summer rice crop needs close attention, and at the same time the commercially important cotton crop, which is planted in April, must be tended during the summer and harvested in September. Wheat and beans then have to be

71 The lake basins and delta lands of the Chang jiang.

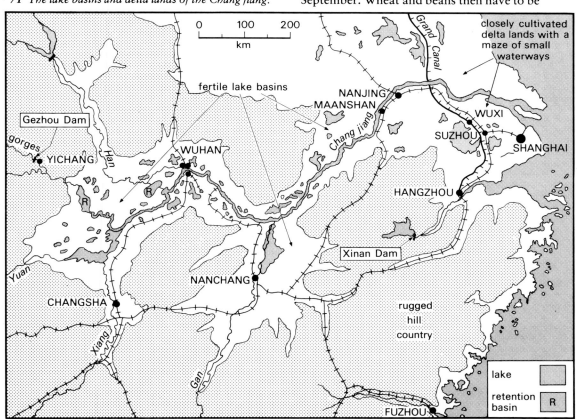

planted ready for harvest in April. County-funded advisory groups visit the villages, and try to see that the best use is made of the soil during a particular season. Decisions have to be made as to which fields should be rested, or receive a particular fertiliser; whether winter beans should follow cotton, or summer beans follow wheat; what proportion of other crops should be grown, whether sweet potatoes, maize, oilseeds or vegetables; how much land should bear fruit crops and other trees; and, of course, how the private plots should be distributed. A great deal of consultation is needed.

The policy of 'where there is water there must be fish' is applied throughout China. Small lakes and ponds are stocked with fish, mainly of the carp family. Here, where lakes abound, fish forms an important part of the diet, and their production is carefully managed: for instance, livestock manure is used to enrich the waters, while fish by-products go to make fertiliser and animal feed (p. 70).

Here, too, the countryside is a blend of older and newer settlements. The older farmsteads of central China usually consist of buildings set about a yard. Most have a single storey, and their flattish roofs are tiled, or sometimes thatched. Many villages and small towns, some of which act as administrative centres, retain their traditional appearance, though with groups of newer brick houses, and long, low workshops and stores. Here and there, new settlements and small factories provide a contrast, though often the local, traditional building styles are used. Even the new bridges, of modern materials, have a typically Chinese appearance, contrasting with the severe functional structures built earlier by the Japanese, or with Russian help.

Here, again, much of the construction work on roads, bridges, canals, small reservoirs and ponds is the responsibility of local counties and townships. In the past, where large projects were required the communes combined to provide labour, even communes from different provinces. For instance, hundreds of thousands of people living in communes in the provinces of Henan, Anhui, and Jiangsu worked together to construct a canal, which extends for hundreds of kilometres, from the hills of eastern Henan to a large lake in the lowlands of Jiangsu. They built pumping-stations to lift water to irrigate dry wheatlands in the hill country. They also constructed many small hydro-electric stations to provide energy for the growing settlements, factories, schools, hospitals and irrigation pumps in each of the provinces. The State provided the larger pumps and the electrical machinery: but the overall project was carried out by local people, working in rotation, so that they could continue to farm their land. They received salaries for their work from their own communes, brigades and teams. Now such plans involve paying a recruited workforce and specialist contractors.

In central China, the rural prosperity, the nature of the produce and the types of local industry vary considerably with the fertility of the land and with distance from a large city. The uplands bordering the Chang jiang lowlands often have a number of specialist activities. Many of the counties in the wooded hill country of western Henan and eastern Sichuan train and employ forestry experts and contract workers and there are many timber factories. Villagers plant tung trees for vegetable oil, and grow huge bamboos for construction, utensils and handicraft products. Forestry is also important in the hill country to the south of the Chang jiang basin, where a great deal of tea comes from plantations which have replaced the smaller, scattered patches of tea bushes.

72 Wherever possible lakes and ponds are stocked with fish. Here, in south-central China, men fish an artificial lake in their factory grounds.

73 Cotton growing in large fields in the Chengling district near Hangzhou.

The Chang Jiang Delta Lands (Yangtze Delta)

Here the flat countryside is crossed by a maze of streams, converted into waterways and linked by thousands of large and small canals. There are many lakes in this huge, flat watery delta, and in the Huai river lowlands to the north. People continually dredge and maintain this network of channels to drain and irrigate the land, and use the waterways for communication. From Hangzhou Bay, south of Shanghai, the Grand Canal runs northwards across the moist landscape (Fig. 123).

Low dykes are built along the channels, and soil is raised into ridges which control the water in the fields. On the seaward side of the delta, large dykes, with sluices to release the water, are built to protect the land. Over the centuries, as the delta has spread, the dykes have been extended eastwards, allowing salty marsh and sandy wastes to be reclaimed for farming. Here cotton is the main commercial crop, for it can tolerate a small amount of salt in the soil. It has been grown by state farms, as well as by village communities.

In the densely populated delta, the old pattern of small family houses lying alongside the waterways remains, although there are also villages and market towns. Despite new houses and increasing mechanisation, there is a feeling of continuity. Small flat boats are still used to carry people and produce along the waterways, and, though there are well organised fisheries, children still fish from the banks. During the hot summer months, lines of men and women work in the wet paddy fields. But, here, too, besides the ever useful cattle and water buffaloes, machines are now used for many of the tasks, and small mechanical pumps lift water to the fields. Large clusters of white ducks are a common sight over the flooded landscape, and when the grain stands high in the fields they swim in the lakes and ponds.

Not all the land is under rice, however. There are stands of tall maize, fields of beans and cotton, patches of sugar cane, fruit trees about the houses, mulberry trees along the banks, and feathery groves of bamboo: so that the low countryside has much variety. The mulberry leaves are fed to silkworms, for though silk production is less important than it was, it is a profitable occupation, particularly associated with certain districts. Two other fibre crops also grow well in this part of China – ramie and jute.

An example of the care taken to ensure that there is as little waste as possible is seen in Fig. 74. This shows, diagrammatically, the land-use in one

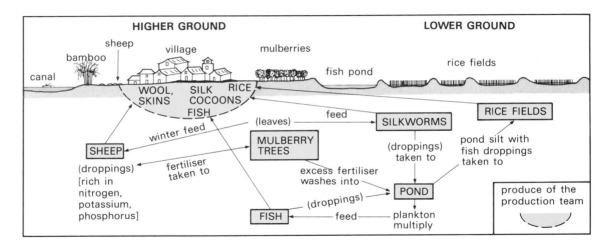

HIGHER GROUND

canal
bamboo
sheep
village
mulberries

WOOL,
SKINS
SILK
COCOONS
FISH
RICE

SHEEP

(droppings)
[rich in
nitrogen,
potassium,
phosphorus]

winter feed

fertiliser
taken to

MULBERRY
TREES

(leaves)

feed

SILKWORMS

(droppings)
taken to

excess fertiliser
washes into

FISH

(droppings)

feed

POND

plankton
multiply

LOWER GROUND

fish pond
rice fields

RICE FIELDS

pond silt with
fish droppings
taken to

produce of the
production team

74 *Ways in which different rural activities in the Chang jiang delta lands support one another and so increase the overall yield of animal and vegetable produce.*

of the villages between Suzhou (Soochow) and Hangzhou (Hangchow), where a number of counties specialise in silkwork breeding, and raise sheep for skins and wool, as a sideline. The sheep, which are fed in winter on mulberry leaves, provide mineral-rich fertiliser for the trees, whose leaves also feed silkworms. Fertiliser from sheep and silkworms enriches the fish ponds, from which fertile bottom mud is removed and spread over the paddy fields. Each occupation helps to increase the yield from another.

The rice and the other summer crops may be followed in autumn by rape, beans, wheat or barley, when, once again, there are decisions to be made about the actual use of each field. County advisors and township cadres ensure that canals and locks are kept in good condition, and the district committees take special care to see that contract farmers cooperate on essential projects. For instance, it is important that everyone should know how to control the water snails which harbour blood flukes and cause disease in humans, and that people are instructed in techniques which can prevent damage by rice-borers. This, of course, is the advantage of a chain of control which runs from the provincial committees, through the counties and townships, to the people themselves.

75 *Fields near Nanjing, in the Chang jiang lowlands, where rice seedlings (Fig. 51) are being transplanted.*

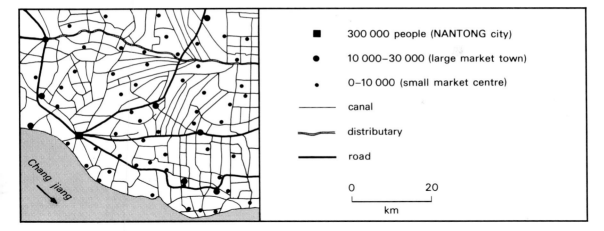

76 *The pattern of settlement north of the main estuary of the Chang jiang.*

In the delta lands, the cotton either goes to the mills in Shanghai or to factories in smaller towns, in the farming areas. Water transport still carries much of the produce: the Grand Canal (p. 120) takes vessels up to 3000 tons. Industrial towns also lie alongside the railways, especially the Shanghai-Nanjing line; and roads thread their way across the lowlands. The traffic is two-way, of course; for, besides sending produce to the city, rural people draw mainly on Shanghai for manufacturers needed for farm purposes and for goods to stock the local stores. Shanghai's factories provide bicycles, sewing machines, garments, radios, TVs, watches, and many of the consumer goods now in demand. The special role of the townships located on the outskirts of Shanghai's urban area is described on p. 136.

Points to Consider

1 The average precipitation of central China is about twice that of the northern plains: it is well spread through the year, but with a summer maximum.

2 Years with a weak monsoon can be very wet ones, and those with a strong monsoon are often unusually dry in the central basin.

3 The moist landscapes of the lowlands of central China are visibly different from those of the northern plains.

4 The use of small mechanical pumps have made water control more effective, and many villages maintain large pump-houses.

5 The larger rural districts in the delta lands have scores of factories making light engineering equipment. Throughout the lowlands local workshops produce semi-mechanised implements.

6 Age-old activities — controlling drainage, irrigation, fish farming, duck rearing and water-transport — combine with scientific controls of water-borne diseases which are common among settlements about the waterways.

7 The central lowlands have particularly benefited from the scientific approach to fish farming, even though this has long provided valuable protein for peasant families.

8 Towns in the delta have a long history of textile production, and large-scale manufacturing followed European commercial activities. Cotton, silk, ramie and wool fibres are all produced locally.

9 Even in the flat areas, soil differences affect the choice of crops. Cotton does well on the lighter calcareous soils; ramie, like rice, is better suited by the clayey water-holding ones.

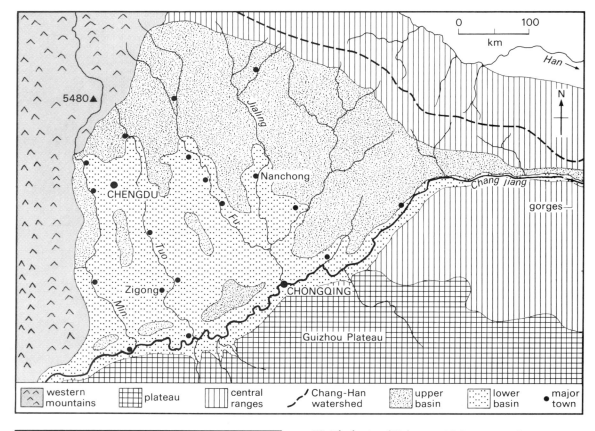

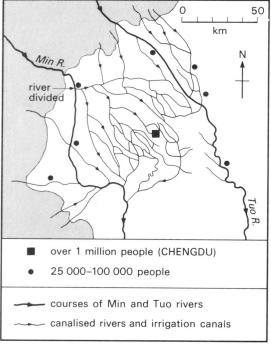

77 The basin of Sichuan, with large rivers flowing southward to the Chang jiang.

78 At Dujiangyan, where the Min river valley broadens, a series of barrages and sluices now divert the waters into different channels. These feed numerous canals which irrigate the plains about Chengdu.

The Sichuan (Szechwan) Basin

In western central China, this large, somewhat higher basin, enclosed by mountain barriers, has a mild climate and a long growing period. Some rural areas are very densely populated, especially the region about Chengdu, where the wide alluvial fans of the river Min spread onto the Chengdu plain, which was once the bed of a large lake. Its deep soils have long been irrigated by a system of water diversion channels, the first of which were established over two thousand years ago. Where the Min emerges from the mountains, its summer torrents spread out, a kilometre wide. Here in the third century BC, its southward-flowing waters were divided by boulder banks, so that half flowed

to the east. These two streams were divided into a
network of channels which irrigated the plains.

An extended network of canals now irrigates
the plainland, which gives an extremely high yield
of rice. Here the summer rice is usually followed
by winter wheat or rape. On the terraced hillsides,
where irrigation water is not available, maize,
soya beans, kaoliang and sweet potatoes are
grown. In fact, there is a great range of crops in
Sichuan. Vegetables and a variety of fruits are
grown throughout the basin, which is known for
its fine oranges; but as physical conditions vary,
certain districts are noted for a particular crop;
some for oilseeds, such as rape or sesame, some
for tobacco, others for cotton. Sugar cane is
grown in many of the valleys, while districts
which include hilly land may cultivate tea or tung
trees, and usually engage in some form of
forestry. Throughout the 'Red Basin', millions of
mulberry trees are planted about the fields and
line the roads and watercourses, especially about
Chengdu. Sichuan has other regions noted for silk

*79 Farm workers divert water through the neatly laid
out mulberry trees from one of the many well-
constructed irrigation channels on the Chengdu plain.*

production; in some the silkworms are fed on the
leaves of oaks, which are common in the lower
parts of the basin.

Streams and rivers cut deeply into the Sichuan
Basin, and spurs of hills also break up the
countryside, which partly account for the variety
of scenery and produce. In the wider, flatter areas,
the rural population usually lives in small
whitewashed, tiled or thatched, houses, set amidst

*80 A settlement south of Chengdu, where every
available piece of land is carefully cultivated. Notice the
precise layout, the neat poles, the shade covering and the
water channel.*

the fields. The other buildings are grouped about a courtyard, where crops are dried and implements stored; they are generally surrounded by fruit trees, which, together with the bamboos, cypress groves, chestnuts and other trees, give the landscape a full green appearance. Small holdings are allotted to the families, most of whom keep hens, ducks and pigs. Large numbers of pigs are reared centrally by collective units, for meat and manure, and for bristles, which are a valuable by-product.

In broken country in the south and west communications are not always easy. Some of the small traditional market towns, with age-old tracks leading to them are now administrative centres serving small hamlets scattered over the landscape. The roads have been much improved however, and in most places, new terracing has increased the area available for crops. While on lowlands the fields are now fewer and larger than they used to be. Many of the settlements are on river terraces, close to waterways, and most of the larger towns have developed as route centres at strategic points along a river.

81 A group of farms in the broken hill country of south-central Sichuan cultivates a variety of crops. There are maize, vegetables, and fruit trees, in the foreground; rice seed beds and flooded paddy fields on the hill terraces; wheat being harvested in the field near the small factory (top, left) and other fields with wheat stubble.

Southern China

The Uplands between the Chang Jiang and Xi Jiang Basins

A variety of uplands separate the basins of the Chang jiang and Xi jiang. Many large and small tributaries to these rivers thread their way, northwards or southwards, through broken hilly

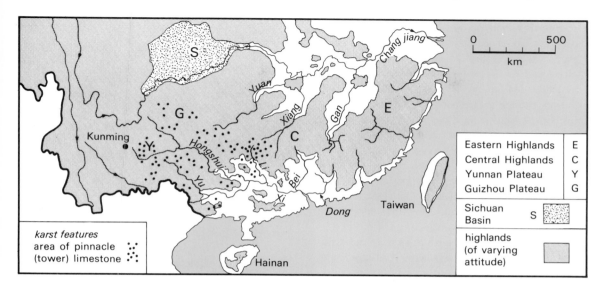

karst features
area of pinnacle
(tower) limestone

Eastern Highlands   E
Central Highlands   C
Yunnan Plateau   Y
Guizhou Plateau   G
Sichuan Basin   S
highlands (of varying attitude)

country, sometimes through quite spectacular scenery.

In the west, in parts of Guizhou, Hunan and Guangxi, there is spectacular karst limestone country, with eroded blocks and dramatic peaks, where arable land is restricted by the broken nature of the landscape. A great deal of rain falls throughout the year, but much of the water sinks into the limestone surface. Small pump-houses are installed to lift water from the rivers to irrigate valley flats, and to bring up water

82 *Highlands from which water runs to the separate river systems of southern China, with an indication of areas where the remains of thick limestones stand as huge pinnacles (Fig. 16).*

83 *An electric pumping station draws water from the Li jiang for the small villages and fields which lie between the great limestone blocks, beyond the graceful bamboos. A packed ferry carries people between villages on either side of the river.*

from wells which tap the abundant underground reserves. Rice is grown in the river valleys, and in level areas where soil has accumulated amid the hills. Many of the people are not Han Chinese; the Zhuang (Chuang) alone number some twelve million, though they mostly live to the south of this region. But, overall, the population of this hill country is sparse. The less steep slopes are closely wooded, so that forestry products are important. The cassia tree, whose name *gui* appears in that of the town Guilin (Kweilin), provides oil for soap and cosmetics. Guilin is one of China's main tourist centres, located amidst the towering karst.

Eastwards lie the hill ranges of northern Guangdong and Fujian, with their steep crests of hard sandstones, and towards the coast are rough granitic hills and igneous rocks. This mountain country is deeply cut by rivers: the rugged coast itself has many drowned river valleys. Here the hot summers and mild winters and the heavy rainfall combine to give a natural forest cover, now much modified. They also allow people to grow rice and a wide variety of other crops, including many tropical fruits, wherever the soils and terrain permit. There is much hillside terracing, but wider arable areas are restricted to the valley floors and to narrow coastlands. However, this hill country has been China's most notable tea-growing region, with exports from ports such as Fuzhou (Foochow) (p. 111). Besides the larger ports, there are numerous small fishing harbours on the drowned inlets along a coast noted for its fine seamen and its many coastal trading vessels.

The South-East Delta Lands

Three rivers contribute to build up the wide delta: the main one is the Xi jiang (West river). This is joined by the Bei jiang (North river), and from the north-east comes the Dong jiang (East river). Across the delta wind a maze of interlacing, meandering distributaries, and an even greater length of man-made canals, maintained by dyking and dredging. Most of the water pours into the sea through the Zhu jiang (Pearl river) estuary. The Xi itself does not drain as large a hinterland as the Chang jiang or Huang He, but the volume of water brought down is large, and even two hundred kilometres upstream the main river is more than a kilometre wide.

Small hills, which were once islands, rise above the farmlands of the flat delta. A grid of power lines supplies the countryside with electricity, and mechanical pumps control the water levels for drainage and irrigation. Here two crops of rice can be grown in a year, with a crop of vegetables between. But, in fact, most of the villages devote a large proportion of their land to vegetables, and, besides rice, grow sugar cane, and fruits such as peaches, lychees, citrus, mangoes, bananas and pineapples.

The farmers near Guangzhou (Canton) can rapidly transport their vegetables, fruit and

84 Tall sugar cane about a typical sturdy, brick-built village near Zhaoqing, west of Guangzhou.

85 *The woman has bought her fish and sugar cane from vendors near the Pearl river bridge, in Guangzhou, and waits for a bus, with other shoppers.*

flowers to the city, where shops and street markets supply the large demand. Some specialise in dairy herds and send milk to the city. Good metalled roads radiate through the countryside and are thronged with urban-rural traffic — with pedestrians, cyclists, pedal carts, horse-drawn vehicles, trucks and buses.

Many of the tens of thousands who move into the city each day have long sugar canes strapped to their bicycles, and cane sellers set up in the busy parts of the city. However, most of the cane from the delta lands goes to local sugar mills or to larger refineries established in rural townships. Most of these towns process other produce in small factories, like those which preserve fruit or make sweets. They also have factories and workshops which make and repair simple machinery.

Refuse from the city is treated and carried to nearby farmlands, together with organic waste and alluvium dredged from the canals. But with such intensive farming, chemical fertilisers are also used to maintain productivity.

Much attention is paid to establishing particular products in certain areas. Some parts of the delta specialise in silkworm culture; while in hill-country west of the delta people rear goats for a special leather. The tropical south-western coastland suits the large-scale production of groundnuts. Across the South China Sea, there is much agricultural and industrial development on the large mineral-rich island of Hainan. With plentiful rainfall, it produces rubber, coconuts,

palm oil, cocoa, coffee, sisal and other tropical produce. It is now a province and the largest of the open economic zones.

Yunnan: The Plateau and the Southern Ranges

In south-western China, far from the densely populated eastern lowlands, areas of highly fertile, closely cultivated land lie among the rugged rocky heights and forested hill ranges. In Yunnan the plateau is dissected by rivers; and below the general level of the surface there are a number of wide basins, where the land has subsided between faults. These contain small rivers and long lakes; some lakes are very large, but others are almost filled by sediments. The alluvial soils on the level floors of these faulted basins are closely farmed, much as the lowlands already described. But the upland blocks which separate the basins are more barren and less easily cultivated. Many of the steeper slopes show the after-effects of forest clearance, and are severely eroded.

The city of Kunming lies in one of the broad basins, which contains a very large lake, Dian Chi. The fields which cover the wide, drained alluvial flats about its shores, produce wheat in winter and rice in summer. Even where the high, steep, fault-bounded hills rise above the waters, there are narrow lakeside fields and vegetable plots. Here lines of houses form long villages, from which fish

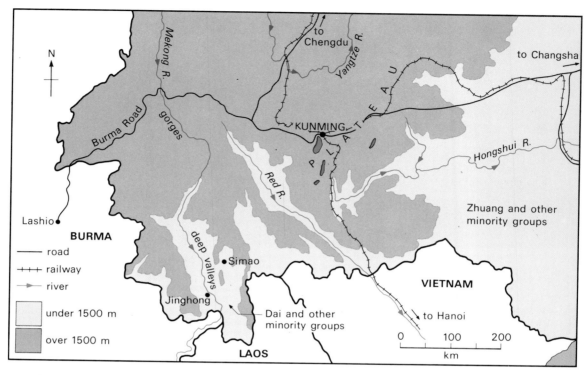

86 The forested south-western mountains and plateau lands of Yunnan.

87 A compact village amid the wheatfields and water channels of the lake basin near Kunming. Notice the nearby vegetable plots, the separate stores and workshops, and the pond. In a few months rice will have replaced this wheat crop.

traps extend into the lake. Red-tiled, brick houses form neat village clusters amid the flat fields and water channels of the broader agricultural areas, where sediments have partly filled the lake. Here and there are larger settlements with machine shops and stores.

This is a mild part of China, where the mean monthly temperatures range from about 10° to 20°C, and allow a long growing period. The lakeside city of Kunming has spread into valleys which open into the basin, and every square metre of available land in its industrial suburbs is given to intensive vegetable growing. Within the city itself, with its wide tree-lined streets, small lakes and landscaped public gardens, any spare land is cultivated in small, neat plots.

Away to the south-west, towards the Burma and Laos borders, ridge after ridge of forested hills alternate with narrow, closely settled valleys. Where some of these widen out, small towns serve a green countryside of rice fields, fruit trees, fields of vegetables and fish ponds bright with water lilies. As in other parts of China, water lilies and lotus plants are harvested from ponds for animal feedstuff, and in the case of lotus, for seeds, which are eaten as a delicacy. Here some of the

88 Cultivation besides Lake Dian Chi, showing the variety of spring crops – yellow rape near the lakeside, wheat to the left, various vegetables, and beans planted on ridges bordering fields later to be flooded. Beyond is an enclosed lagoon, stocked with fish.

89 A Dai home in a village near Jinghong, in Yunnan. The living rooms are on a platform, with decorative plants in pots (a common sight in China), and storage space beneath. Bananas grow in the compound.

valley sides are cleared for tea bushes, and lines of rubber trees run along the lower slopes.

There are a large number of Dai (Thai) people and other minority groups in the south-west. Their style of clothing and housing are traditional. The Chinese government officially encourages minority peoples to keep their identity; though the Han Chinese closely direct their affairs, despite the minority representation in local, regional government.

Their agriculture and social organisation is much the same as in other parts of China. This can be seen in the villages about the small market town of Jinghong, which lies on a broad, flat terrace above the river Mekong. Here the main valley opens to allow a wide area of cultivation, amid forested hills. The fertile farmland includes many Dai villages, with their houses of

90 A village collective east of Jinhong keeps several hundred buffaloes for meat: here some are watered in a shallow village lake.

wood and bamboo. In each, the main rooms and surrounding balcony are on a platform raised above a space used for storage and animal compounds. Production is concentrated on rearing animals for meat – herds of buffaloes, and pigs – and on their large plantations of bananas and sugar cane. Timber products and kapok come from the forest; and timber and bamboos are rafted down the Mekong, and carried up the steep banks to the villages above.

Even in this remote region there is now more mechanisation; large and small tractors are housed in the villages, and pumps are used for water extraction and spraying. Young people are trained in machine maintenance and electrical work. There is a generous allocation of land for family produce, and the early morning street market in Jinghong is thronged with colourful family groups with their vegetables, spices, and livestock, with stalls offering packeted goods and people cooking local food.

Small industries are evident: machine shops, timber working, women finishing textiles and packing kapok. In the town itself the state administration is seen in the concrete offices, agricultural institute and cinema (thronged in the evenings), which starkly contrast with the local style of the family houses and secondary school buildings. Power comes to the town from a small hydro-electric station in a nearby valley.

The differences between this remote, forested part of China and the light grey hills of the loess lands are immense; yet there are striking similarities in the organised ways of life of their rural populations, even though languages and customs differ.

91 A Dai village set in closely wooded country east of Jinghong. Apart from tending herds and the main cash crops families grow vegetables (Fig. 59) and tropical fruits like pawpaw (papaya) (right), and keep pigs and chickens. Bamboo is used for fencing, and the timber comes from local forests.

Points to Consider

1 The many contrasts in the vegetation and types of farming in the Sichuan basin reflect local variations in topography and climate.
2 The water supply systems about Chengdu show a long continuity of development so often seen in China.
3 In the broken hill country of the Sichuan basin, the scattered family houses about the administrative townships form a different pattern of settlement to that on the plains.
4 The karst limestone country generally receives adequate rainfall for farming, but has its own problems of water supply.
5 The forms of land-use and the marketing arrangements of the settlements of the Xi river delta clearly show the influences of a great city.
6 Farmers in southern Yunnan have much the same marketing arrangements as those in northern China, though what they produce is very different.
7 The bustling activity in the free markets of small towns shows the importance of private plots and incentive schemes to the families and the community.

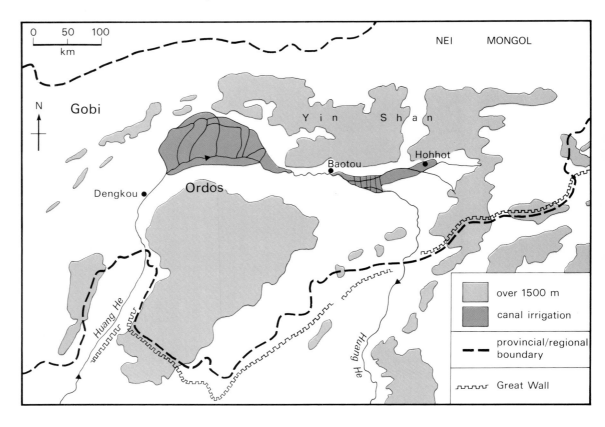

92 *Dry country about the great northern bends of the Huang He, whose waters are diverted for canal irrigation.*

93 *Milking goats on the Tian Shan. These Kazakh herders are semi-nomadic and, as suggested by the surrounds of the skin tent, remain close to good grazing for months at a time.*

The Far Interior

Nei Mongol (Inner Mongolia)

This autonomous region stretches from the forested mountains of the north-east westwards across a plateau which stands, on the average, some thousand metres above sea-level. It becomes progressively drier towards the west and north, where much of it is a desert plain, with inland drainage and seasonal lakes, some of which provide salt and soda. Its smooth rock surface is covered with sands and gravel, or with angular stones, and deserves the descriptive Mongolian name, *Gobi*, a waste.

However, much of the central and eastern parts are a dry steppe grassland, where livestock herding has been the traditional activity. The rainfall is erratic, and winter temperatures fall to as low as −40°C.

The wide tableland rises gently southward to a rim of mountains, the Yin Shan. These fall steeply to the south where the Huang He flows

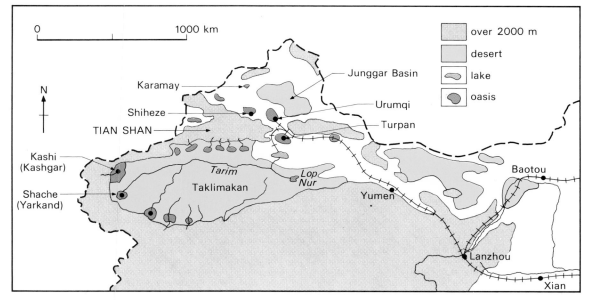

94 Irrigated settlements about the dry basins and developed mineral sources in Xinjiang, and the key rail link with the eastern cities.

plateau rises gently to a rim of mountains, the Yin eastwards. Here, on the fertile clayey soils of the irrigated alluvial plains, are the most populated areas. The Hetao plains, to the north of the river, are irrigated for spring wheat and oats, and millet and kaoliang are grown as dry crops. Here oilseeds, such as sesame, castor, rape and linseed, and also sugar beet, are grown as cash crops. Water is diverted from the Huang He by a dam at Dengkou. South of this is the dry Ordos region, separated from the main loess lands by hill ranges, along which runs the ruins of the Great Wall.

Further east, the Yin Shan ranges shelter another irrigated plain, where the capital, Hohhot, once a regional centre for Mongolian herdsmen, has become a small industrial city, with steelworks, and textile and sugar beet factories. The population of these irrigated lands, and of the large steel centre, Baotou, is mainly Han Chinese, who form the majority of Nei Mongol's twenty million people.

There are some two million Mongol people. About a sixth of them have been, and many still are, semi-nomadic pastoralists, moving their flocks of sheep and goats, their cattle, horses, and, perhaps, camels from winter to summer pastures. Some, in the crop raising areas, practise summer herding and winter stall-feeding. The family

dwelling of the nomadic people is the *yurt*, which has layers of felt covering a circular framework of willow trellis, about four metres in diameter and a metre high; today they may well use a plastic framework.

Their movements are now restricted: many of the pasturelands have been fenced, and irrigation systems have been installed, to encourage settlement. About three-quarters of the pastoralists are administered through the equivalent of county units, called 'banners', which are related to tribal groups; while others have become part of agricultural communities. The management of their grazing lands has been aimed at improving the livestock, but is also designed to control movement in a part of China which is a delicate border region, between Mongolia and the USSR.

The Oases of Xinjiang-Uygur

These oases lie in the basins of Chinese central Asia, hemmed in by snowy ranges. The scale is difficult to imagine, for the Tarim basin alone is nearly 1300 km long and over 600 km at its widest. At the centre are the sands of the Taklimakan (Takla Makan) desert. The only river, the Tarim, runs along the northern side of the basin and into the salt flats which form part of the drainage towards the saline lake, Lop Nur (Lop Nor). But streams cascade down from the melting snows on the mountains and cross coarse

alluvial deposits before they sink into the desert sands. The mountain waters themselves have brought down this gravelly material, which spreads outwards from the lower slopes in wide fans.

Small oasis towns developed where these waters were used to irrigate the alluvial fans, and through them passed the ancient trade routes which

95 The karez system of irrigation which is widely used about the rims of the western basins. The underground channel CC carries groundwater from beneath the foothills to irrigate arid lowland.

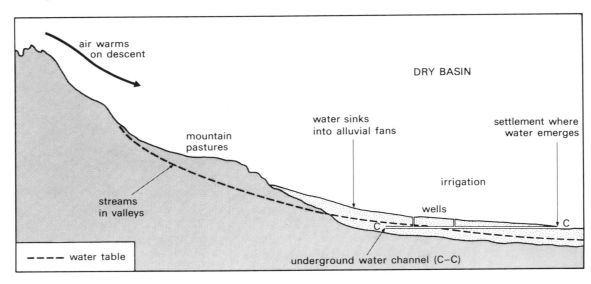

96 *The Turpan oasis, where irrigation provides the contrast between arid, eroded hillsides and the lines of trees and currant yielding vines.*

The lower Turpan (Turfan) depression to the north-east has greater extremes of temperature. But, here too, the surface waters and underground sources are controlled to provide irrigation for cotton, and in the sunny, hot summers, the people grow apricots, peaches, melons and grapes.

The large Junggar basin (Dzungaria basin) to the north of the Tian Shan is not quite as arid. Much of it has sufficient grass for the flocks and herds of the nomadic Kazakh families, and some of the mountain slopes have close spruce forest up to the tree limit. The State Construction Corps and people from the communes combined to build mountain reservoirs, control the river waters and tap underground sources, so that there are now extensive areas of irrigated arable farming, with much cotton growing. Almost a million people live in the area about Shiheze, to the west of Urumqi, below the slopes of the Tian Shan. Most of them are Han people who have been moved westward; many of them directed here from the eastern cities. Here fields in the foothills grow wheat and maize, and the reservoirs supply water to the adjacent lowland through more than ten thousand kilometres of irrigation canals. Cotton, sugar cane and oilseeds are all processed in Shiheze

The development of mineral resources in this part of Xinjiang has changed the whole way of life and the composition of the population, bringing Han technicians and workers into an area once primarily occupied by Uygur, Kazakh and other tribal minorities. The development of the new oilfields (p. 92), the coal and iron production (p. 102) and the steelworks and manufacturing at Urumqi, with the consequent increases in population, have made it essential to increase agricultural production. In oases about the city, a canal network supplies water to hundreds of thousands of hectares of farmland which sends fresh produce daily to the city, as well as producing the kind of cash crops mentioned above. State investment has been used to canalise the local river and line it with concrete to prevent seepage, and to generate the electric energy which

followed the northern and southern edges of the basin. Some towns, like Kashi (Kashgar) and Shache (Yarkand) became large trading centres, controlling routes to other parts of Asia.

After 1949, the Chinese formed a Production and Construction Corps to make the most of the water reserves of the high snowfields, and to use groundwater from within the basin. On the north side of the basin, in particular, they built reservoirs and canals to make better use of the meltwater, and dug long underground channels (karez) to conduct ground-water from the foot of the mountains to irrigate flat areas with good soils. Communes were established, and also more highly mechanised *state farms*. The land near the sides of the basins have considerable climatic advantage in winter, for the air which rises over the mountains and sinks into the basin is warmed during its descent, so that there is not the extreme cold which affects so many parts of Central Asia. There is also a long growing period, of some 220 days. This enables people to grow wheat, maize, rice, kaoliang, barley, peas and beans by irrigation, and cotton and sugar cane are now important commercial crops; here, again, cotton's tolerance of slightly salty soils is an advantage.

97 A canal runs through an expanding industrial suburb of Urumqi, where tall chimneys indicate textile factories. The arid foothills of the Tian Shan stand out in the background.

pumps groundwater into storages. Such developments help to provide food for the growing city; but supplies are also brought in by road and rail from eastern China.

The population of Xinjiang, now some fourteen million, has been boosted by the inflow of Han Chinese to this agriculturally and industrially developing Autonomous Region. However, the Uygur (Uighur) tribal people, of Moslem faith, who once dominated these interior basins, still make up more than half the population. Their relationships with the Han Chinese have been strained; this is partly due to differences in social and religious behaviour, partly to differences in occupations, and also to the desire of sections of the Han population to return to the eastern parts of China.

Lhasa and the Valleys of High Tibet (Xizang)

The climate in the valley of the Gyi Qu river in which Lhasa is situated, and in the main Zangbo (Tsangpo) valley, is milder than that of the high plateaus; but, even so, the temperatures can rise in summer to over 30°C and fall in winter to below −20°C, and the growing season is only 140 days long.

Under the old feudal system, the chief grain crop, highland barley, was grown by serf labour. The incoming Han Chinese, who supply most of the capital for the Tibetan AR, at first organised small communes and state farms. They developed special strains of winter wheat to suit the conditions, and improved varieties of tomatoes, cabbages, peas, turnips, potatoes and apples, giving a much greater choice of crops to suit the restricted areas of arable land. Rape and sugar beet have also been introduced, and are grown on the state farms. Pigs and hardy breeds of cattle have been added to the traditional farm animals, sheep, goats and yaks, which ranged fairly widely over sparse grazing land, but can now benefit from fodder crops. But there are still groups of

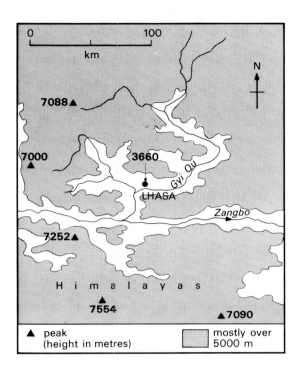

98 *The valleys about Lhasa amid these high Tibetan ranges are able to support summer grains and vegetables, at over 3600 m.*
99 *A view from the great Potala monastery across some of the more recent extensions of Lhasa and the Gyi Qu valley.*

semi-nomadic herdsmen living with their families in yak-wool tents, or in small stone cottages, on the high plateaus.

Most tasks on the family farms are still carried out by hand. Tractors and combine harvesters used on the larger farms are sent in parts from the east, and reassembled. Lhasa is still a remote city, ten days by truck from Sichuan; through there is an airport, and a railway is being built across the mountains and plateaus from Lanzhou.

There has always been a fuel shortage and, in the absence of wood, dried dung has provided heat for cooking. Fuel for machinery is brought from the east, and an oil pipeline now runs from Lanzhou to Lhasa. The Chinese have built small hydro-electric stations, which help local manufacturing. Many goods used locally are produced in small factories and workshops, such as processed foods, footwear, woollen textiles, farm implements and batteries. There are projects for solar, wind, and geothermal energy.

There are now some 200000 people in the city itself; but the new western extension houses mainly Han Chinese. Many have come to reorganise the agriculture and construct dams, roads, school and other buildings. During the Cultural Revolution large numbers were drafted here to work on the land. There is still a gap between the Tibetan people and the new arrivals.

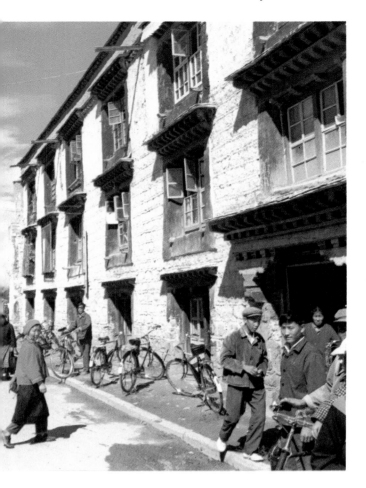

Most Tibetans live in the old parts of the city. Many retain their old faith, even though Lamaism, the Tibetan form of Buddhism, was officially eradicated and most of the monasteries closed during the Cultural Revolution. In accordance with state policy towards minority peoples, there are efforts to strengthen the teaching of the Tibetan language and to preserve the local culture. Some monasteries are being restored, and the great Potala monastery of the Dalai Lama can now be visited. Thousands of Tibetan teachers have been trained in eastern China; this, of course, makes for a new literate generation of Tibetans, but, in fact, steers them away from the past cultures of their homeland and towards the broad ideals of the new China, so tensions remain.

100 Summer sunshine on partly renovated buildings in the older part of Lhasa.

101 A dam across the Dadu river in mountainous western Sichuan, with its sluice gates and spillway and a power station which supplies energy to the many industries being developed down-valley.

Points to Consider

1 Life in each of these Autonomous Regions shows the tensions which can develop between local minority peoples and the Han Chinese who have come to form the majority of the population.
2 There is much evidence of increasing material prosperity in these ARs, compared with life in the past, as there is throughout China.
3 There are still different life-styles between people of different origins.
4 In each of these ARs there are problems due to climatic causes, but people who are now the main minority established ways of life which came to terms with their difficult environment.

5 Each AR has areas where the population is particularly concentrated.
6 Religion has played a central role in the life of these minority peoples, either forms of Buddhism or the Moslem faith. These came under pressure as people with no state religion became dominant.
7 China gains by developing and creating a stable, settled population in these strategic regions.
8 Mineral wealth is a great spur to development of more remote places, and encourages agricultural improvements.
9 Improved communications have been made a priority for Xinjiang and Tibet.

4 Modern China: Developing the Energy Resources

Meeting Energy Demands

The demands for electricity continue to increase as power is needed for the towns and cities and large manufacturing industries, for the growing number of small factories and processing plants spread throughout the country, for the rural settlements, and for pumps which drain or irrigate so much of the farmland. Large power stations feed electric grid systems supplying the cities and main industrial areas. But China is too large a country for an overall, fully-linked grid system. Numerous small individual power systems, fed by local generators, supply electricity to the rural areas and less-developed parts of the country.

The drive towards industrialisation and modernisation has been checked in some areas by power shortages. The energy potential is great. But China looks for more efficient production and distribution of its coal resources, and has sought foreign investments and expertise to help develop hydro-electric schemes and search for new oil sources.

Coal

Most of the power stations are coal-burning, though not all. The large coalfields of the north and north-east send coal by rail and water to the northern and eastern industrial cities and coastal city-ports. The rivers and canals carry a great deal of coal. But, as Fig. 102 shows, there are numerous large and small coalfields in other parts of China, and there are many places where mining on a small scale, supplies local power stations.

China's reserves of coal are very large indeed, with particularly extensive deposits in the north. Some immensely thick seams of black coal lie in the three provinces of the north-east (1), where there is highly mechanised mining. They feed power stations in the industrial areas and also supply coking coal to the region's iron and steel industries (p. 103). The country's greatest output is from these north-eastern fields, which also send coal southwards to other parts of the country by railways and coastal shipping. Thick oilshales,

102 China's main coalfields in regions 1–4 have immense resources; but the many other, smaller fields have great local importance.

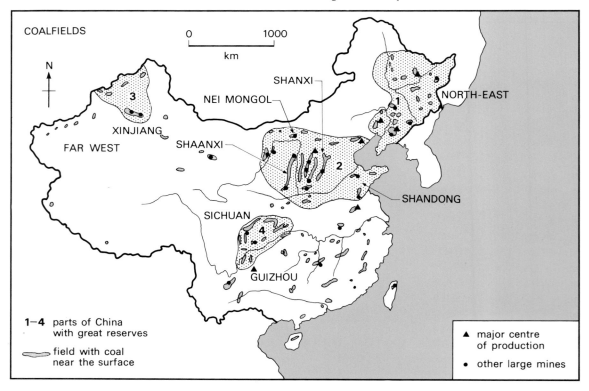

COALFIELDS

0   1000
km

N

SHANXI

NEI MONGOL

3

XINJIANG

FAR WEST

SHAANXI

NORTH-EAST

1

2

SHANDONG

SICHUAN

4

GUIZHOU

1–4 parts of China with great reserves

field with coal near the surface

▲ major centre of production

• other large mines

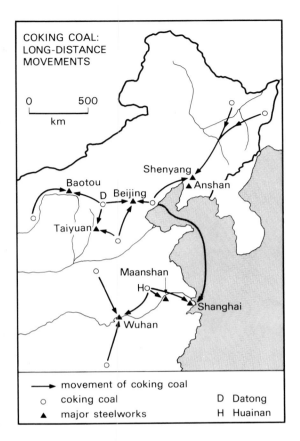

COKING COAL:
LONG-DISTANCE
MOVEMENTS

0   500
    km

Shenyang
Baotou
D Beijing ▲Anshan
Taiyuan
Maanshan
H○
▲Shanghai
▲Wuhan

→ movement of coking coal
○ coking coal   D Datong
▲ major steelworks   H Huainan

103 In the north the railways mainly move the coking coal to large steelworks. In central and southern China inland and coastal shipping is additionally important, and waterways also carry coal to power stations (Fig. 105).

locomotive manufacturing town Datong further north. Fields to the west of the Shandong peninsula are really an extension of these northern coalfields.

Far to the west, near Urumqi (3), in Xinjiang, there are massive reserves in a region where industrial development has followed both the completion of the long railway from the east and the increasing production from its oilfields. Coal also lies beneath the red sandstones of Sichuan (4). Seams are exposed where the rivers cut into the sandstones, and there are outcrops on the margin of the Red Basin. Mining has greatly increased here in recent years.

Coal also occurs in the hill country which separates the Huang He basin from the central lowlands of the Chang jiang. Here mines supply cities in eastern central China and send coal to ports on the Chang jiang, and to the heavy industrial city of Wuhan, which also gets coal from the south. The coal reserves of southern China, however, are well below those of the north; nevertheless, there is coal in all the provinces, and sufficient in Guizhou to plan large-scale exports to Europe. The annual total from the many small mines in southern China is perhaps a quarter of the country's production. The local value of these small mines is very great indeed, though the mining methods are often very crude compared with those of the larger mines.

104 Factories along the eastern side of the Fen valley, in a coal-mining district south of Taiyuan, with spoil tips above.

which lie above the coal in a number of the fields, are also mined and distilled, for oil and oil products, notably at Fushun (Fig. 120).

There are even more extensive coal deposits in Shanxi (Shansi), Shaanxi (Shensi) and the adjoining provinces, and in Ningxia and Nei Mongol (Inner Mongolia) (2). Much of it lies beneath thick sandstones. But in Shanxi there is joint-venture open-cast mining with an American company, and near-surface north—south fields lying either side of the Huang He are highly productive. When China began its drive to industrialise during the 1950s, railways were extended to open up and serve the mines and growing factory towns, like Taiyuan and others in the Fen He valley, and the

105 Three coal barges abreast on the Chang jiang at Chongqing. Coal is mined within the city boundaries and along the Jialing valley to the north. Thermal power stations supply much of the city's electricity.

China's policy of combining old methods and modern ones, and small industries with large ones, in order to overcome shortages, is known as 'walking on two legs'. This aptly applies to the coal industry; for though there has been a great drive to introduce mechanisation, with the help of imported coal-mining equipment, in order to increase the production from the big mines, there is also a policy of opening new, small mines and using the abundant man-power to produce coal without the help of modern equipment. This ties up with the increase in the number of small coal-burning power stations.

The railways have been something of a bottleneck in coal distribution. Investments in double-tracking and electrification aim to speed up the transport of coal to export ports and key industrial regions.

Petroleum and Oil Shales

In the 1950s China made great efforts, with Russian help, to develop oilfields, especially in the far west; even so, it still imported most of the oil it required from the USSR. After the break with Russia, it was essential to find and develop new oilfields, wherever this seemed possible. China succeeded so well that it became self-sufficient in most of the types of oil needed by industry, and by 1972 was exporting oil to Japan.

Oil exports also earn other foreign currency, which the country needs so much. But as China uses more trucks and tractors, more diesel on the railways, develops more petro-chemical and other oil-consuming industries, and as the standards of living of the growing population improve, home demands are likely to make it more difficult to keep up the exports which bring in these earnings. On the other hand, China has, for the time being, shaken off its dependency on imported oil, and is enlisting foreign aid to find new sources.

Fig. 106 shows the main oil-producing fields. Those at Karamay, in the semi-arid Junggar basin in the far west of Xinjiang (1), have a large

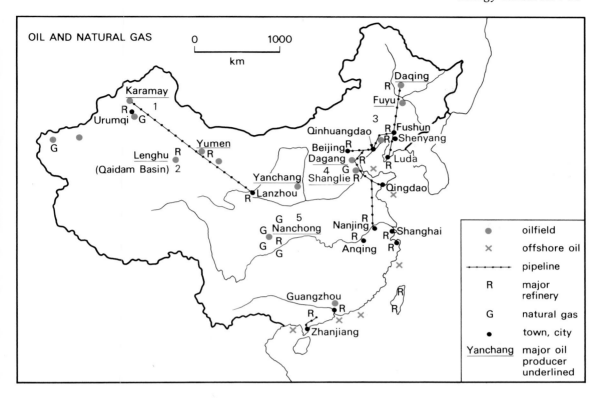

OIL AND NATURAL GAS

0   1000

km

●	oilfield
✕	offshore oil
•·•·•·	pipeline
R	major refinery
G	natural gas
●	town, city
Yanchang	major oil producer underlined

106 China is now an oil-exporter; but as production from inland fields levels off and home demands grow, the development of proved off-shore sources is a priority.

output; oil is piped to refineries 150 km to the south. There are other producing fields near Urumqi and in the Tarim basin, and finds are still being made. The excess oil from these regions is piped eastwards to refineries at Yumen, which lies close to other productive fields (2). Yumen is also linked by pipeline to the very large refineries at Lanzhou (Lanchow), which send oil products eastwards by rail. Both Yumen and Lanzhou manufacture oil-surveying and drilling equipment. As Fig. 106 shows, there is another important western oilfield, in the Qaidam (Tsaidam) basin.

As a result of the efforts in the 1960s, the oil basin discovered beneath the plains of north-east China (3) proved to be among the most productive, especially the field at Daqing (Taching). This supplies its own enormous refinery and pipes oil southwards to other refineries, like those at the petro-chemical town of Liaoyang, south of Shenyang; its oil is also

shipped through the port of Luda (Dalian). The name Daqing (Great Joy) reflects its importance to China; but there are already signs that production here has reached its peak, and, like all petroleum reserves, must decline. Hence new

107 The plan of a new village, Bojishan, about an oil-well near Daqing, showing the landscaping and use of lakes on the flat marshy plain. It also emphasises the development of separate agricultural communities in these Heilongjiang oilfields (p. 140).

finds, like those in southern Liaoning (Fig. 120), are important. Prospects elsewhere are promising. Oil occurs beneath the Huang He delta and the plain inland of the Gulf of Bohai. In 1970, large-scale production began at Shanglie, near the mouth of the Huang He; and oil is piped to Beijing and Tianjin from the fields at Dagang, south-east of Tianjin. Pipelines carry some of the excess oil to Qingdao on the Shandong peninsula, where it is received by oil tankers. Other pipelines carry oil southwards to Nanjing (Nanking); and river craft take it on to Wuhan and Shanghai. There is thus a complete pipeline linkage from Daqing, in the far north, to the lower Chang jiang (Yangtze kiang).

The major searches and developments, however, are likely to be off the coasts. Offshore oil is already coming from wells in the Gulf of Bohai, and from others off the estuary of the Pearl river, and in the Beibu Wan (Gulf of Tonking) in the South China Sea. China has undertaken joint exploration and development with foreign investors, and aims to make use of foreign capital and technology; the benefits are shared by the partners, though China keeps careful control of the resources. The reserves of offshore oil and gas appear to be very large, and their development will greatly help China's plans for modernisation.

Another oil basin is being worked in central Sichuan (5), some 200 km north of Chongqing (Chungking). Such reserves are particularly valuable in inland regions, for transport by road, rail or pipeline is costly in a large country like China.

The distillation of China's oil shales also yields large quantities of oil. Oil shales are abundant in the north-east (p. 107) and in the coal basins near Datong; they are also mined and treated far to the south, in the south-west of Guangdong province, and in the western interior, near Urumqi. The Sichuan basin not only mines and distils oil shales, but is the country's chief producer of natural gas.

Natural Gas

There are great reserves of natural gas still to be developed. It is associated with some of the oilfields, as at Dagang. But the greatest concentration is in Sichuan, where it is piped to fertiliser factories, burnt as fuel in iron- and steel-works and other industries, and also used for household purposes and for running public buses. There are plans to pipe it to other parts of China.

Hydro-Electric Energy

'Walking on Two Legs'

China has enormous hydro-electric power potential, especially in the south. But many of the likely sites for hydro-electric stations are far from the cities and large industrial areas. Large hydro-electric projects involve enormous construction expense, for equipment and materials, skilled engineering and labour. The very large developments described below are part of multi-purpose schemes designed to create dams, lakes and canals for flood control and irrigation, as well as to produce electricity. Despite the use made of the abundant labour available in China, these projects are still immensely expensive for a developing country.

But again, southern China, in particular, demonstrates the policy of 'walking on two legs', for numerous small hydro-electric stations have been built to supply local needs, and are sometimes combined with coal-burning stations to feed a local network of power-lines. In rural areas, water-power is used to turn tiny generators to supply electricity at the village level.

Fig. 108 shows the location of large multi-purpose hydro-electric schemes and of other regionally important medium-to-large hydro-electric stations. It also gives a general indication of those parts of the country where electricity is often supplied by very tiny hydro-electric generators.

The North and North-East

In the north-east (1) there are several dams with large hydro-electric stations on the Songhua (Sungari) and its tributaries, which run northwards to the Heilong jiang, and on the southward flowing rivers. These create reservoirs large enough to overcome the problems of freezing during the bitter winters. The electricity produced boosts the large quantities of energy obtained

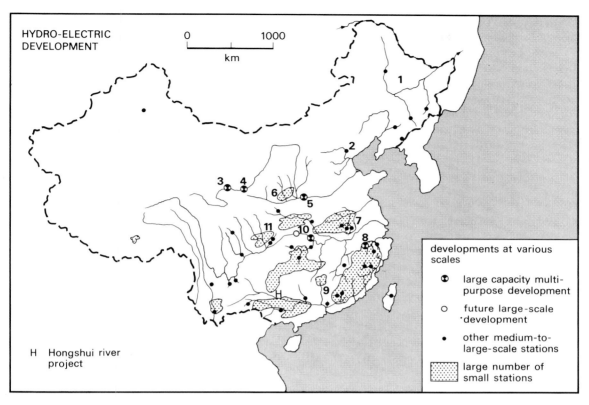

HYDRO-ELECTRIC
DEVELOPMENT

0   1000

km

developments at various
scales

  ⊗   large capacity multi-
         purpose development

  ○   future large-scale
         ·development

  •   other medium-to-
         large-scale stations

         large number of
         small stations

H   Hongshui river
project

108 *There is great power potential in the high
mountains and moist south-west, but these are far from
the well-populated eastern industrial areas. There are
many very small generators on streams in rural areas
(notably in the shaded regions).*

109 *The Huang He flows through the large city of
Lanzhou, whose many industries benefit from the
hydro-electricity generated upstream in the Liujia gorge.*

from coal, and supplies the big industrial regions of the north-east.

There are flood-control dams on many of the rivers draining to the Gulf of Bohai, and some form deep lakes. One of these supplies Beijing with water and also generates electricity for the city and its surroundings (2); and another, larger, multi-purpose dam is being constructed on the Luanhe, 190 km north-east of the city, near the Great Wall.

The Huang He Basin

The nature of the Huang He and the reasons for its developments are described on p. 12. The first of its huge hydro-electric stations (3) is below a dam built across the Longyang gorge, cut into the high surface some 250 km west of Lanzhou (Lanchow). Its energy supplies eastern Qinghai and Xining's industries. Even here, the volume of water above the dam fluctuates greatly between the winter low and summer maximum from year to year. The importance of flood-control is shown by another scheme 80 km up-river of Lanzhou, where a huge reservoir has been formed in the Liujia gorge, behind the high retaining wall of a second multi-purpose dam (4). During flood periods it is able to reduce the maximum river flow by some 40 per cent. Its generators provide electricity for the million inhabitants of Lanzhou and its heavy industries. The electric grid extends over a wide area of farmland, which also benefits from the waters supplied for irrigation. Some 300 km down-river, another dam mainly serves to supply an irrigation system; it also helps to improve the river navigation.

Far to the east, in the loess lands, the waters of the Wei river join the Huang He, which then flows through a series of gorges. Here the Sanmen dam (5) has been built across the main river Fig. 12. This huge multi-purpose project is the key to the flood control and irrigation schemes in the middle and lower parts of the north China plains. It was planned to have an output of electricity of more than a million kilowatts; but the long lake behind the dam received so much yellow silt, which pours into it during the summer flood period, that in four years its storage capacity was reduced by 40 per cent.

Tunnels have been cut in one wall of the gorge to allow silt-choked water to surge through, and the dam's sluices are opened to allow flood waters quickly to be discharged down-stream. Towards the end of summer, the main reservoir is topped up with clearer water. The dam still acts as an emergency flood control and still holds immense amounts of water for use in the dry season; but the electrical generating capacity, though large, is now reduced. Other advantages have been lost. In flood, a flow of clear water below the dam would have been able to erode the river bed and deepen the channel, thus lessening the possibility of flooding downstream. The age-old policy of building the dykes ever higher, to prevent flooding, not only increases the dangers should a breach occur, but interferes with the more recent siphoning systems built to take water from the river to irrigate the surrounding, lower land; so that anything which deepens the channel is a tremendous advantage. In some stretches, dredging boats are now used as an alternative to further dyke raising: their hydraulic cannons disturb the silt, which is removed by pumps.

The problems can only really be solved by methods which will ensure that the many tributaries of the Wei and Huang He carry a much smaller load of silt. Already many of the

110 Powerlines cross the Huang He near Zhengzhou, where the muddy water is pumped up to settling beds and then fed to irrigation systems and water-supply pipelines.

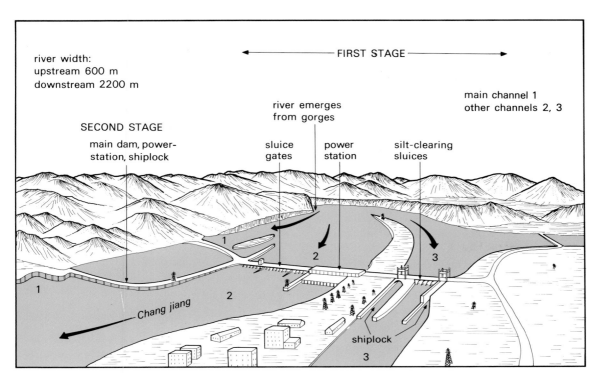

river width:
upstream 600 m
downstream 2200 m

— FIRST STAGE —

main channel 1
other channels 2, 3

river emerges
from gorges

SECOND STAGE
main dam, power-
station, shiplock

sluice
gates

power
station

silt-clearing
sluices

1

2

3

1

2

Chang jiang

shiplock

3

111 The site of the Gezhou Dam below the Chang jiang gorges, where three channels are being harnessed – Nos. 2 and 3 being developed first, as described in the text. (Source: China Reconstructs. *vol XXX (10), p. 8).*

numerous small control dams built across minor streams and rivers have become useless, for the reasons given above. They are now unable to stand up to flood conditions. Efforts are being made to prevent the serious erosion which supplies such a heavy load of material to the streams. The slopes are terraced; drainage channels, small control dams and reservoirs are carefully supervised and cleared as far as possible; and millions upon millions of trees are being planted throughout the loess lands. Fig. 177 shows the plans for a 'second Great Wall' of trees, with branching belts to run for a total of 7000 km through the whole of the 'danger lands' of northern China.

Electric energy is also generated at smaller dams on the Wei, and on other rivers draining to the Huang He (6). The larger of them were constructed jointly by the state and local communes, and help to supply electricity throughout these important farmlands.

The Chang Jiang Gorges and Gezhou Dam

One of China's greatest projects is the control of the Chang jiang as it swirls through the gorges in the mountainous region on the border of Sichuan and Hubei (10). The Gezhou dam has been built just upstream of Yichang (Ichang), where the river leaves the Xiling gorge. It provides energy and ranks with the world's largest hydro-electric developments. The energy created will greatly help the economic progress of the mineral-rich province of Sichuan, which already uses its own coal and gas in thermal stations, and has a number of moderate size hydro-electric stations on its southward-flowing rivers (11). The Gezhou dam is also able to provide sufficient energy to overcome the shortages which have hampered production at the steel mills at Wuhan (p. 111). The dam can only check a small proportion of summer torrents, but any dam is important, for flood control in the central basins of the Chang jiang has relied partly on the absorbing effects of wide overflow basins (p. 14), and these have gradually become less effective. Ship elevators at the dam, instead of the usual locks, enable vessels of 10 000 tonnes to sail up river to Chongqing (Chungking).

The Gezhou dam is sited where two islands divide the river into three channels. Dams, sluices, a power station and the shiplock were first completed across two of the channels, and the main channel blocked off, for another power station and shiplock to be built. The large amount of silt brought down from the upper river basin can be cleared through the main sluice gates, with the help of special water-churning sluices, shown in the diagram. The power stations feed energy into a regional network of power lines. A further scheme is planned for other dams to be sited upstream in the gorges, creating even deeper water up-river.

Downriver at Wuhan, the Chang jiang is joined by the Han Shui. The Han valley is followed by power lines from a thermal station in Henan province, and hydro-electricity is also generated on the upper river.

Large and Small Stations in the East

In eastern China much has been done to control the waters which drain from the hill country to the Huai lowlands (7). Many flood-control dams have been built and some have sizeable hydro-electric stations. Much further south, beyond the Chang jiang delta, a very large hydro-electric station has been built at the Xinan dam, in the northern part of the south-eastern uplands (Fig. 71). This supplies the electric grid which serves Hangzhou, Shanghai, Nanjing, and other cities.

Similarly, rivers in the hill country of the south-east are harnesssed to supply the grid serving Guangzhou and the Xi jiang delta (9). The larger stations are shown in Fig. 108, but there are many smaller ones; one river has a series of nine small-to-medium size hydro-electric stations below a reservoir high in the hills. In the counties about Meizhou, in eastern Guangdong, there are hundreds of small hydro-electric generators.

Developments in the South and South-West

These hilly parts of China also have a large, hydro-electric potential, but their rural regions have mainly depended on tiny generators. Larger hydro-electric projects are now in progress in Yunnan, however, and several of the ten dams to be built on the Hongshui (Fig. 108) are already helping the economic development of southern China.

112 *A small hydro-electric station in the forested hill country in south-west Yunnan, a region of great power potential but remote from the main population concentrations.*

Nuclear Energy

The Chinese at first concentrated most of their nuclear energy developments in the arid north-west, just to the east of the salt-lake Lop Nur (Lop Nor). There are nuclear research establishments and industrial production of nuclear materials at Baotou, in the Nei Mongol (Inner Mongolia) AR, and at Lanzhou, where energy from the great Luijia dam is available.

China is now building nuclear power stations in the coastal south-east. That at Daya Bay near the Hong Kong border, is to supply the Shenzhen Special Economic Zone (p. 112) and export energy to Hong Kong. China is now a major nuclear power, even though it is a 'developing country' which has had to wrestle with problems of rural poverty as serious as those in other less developed countries; this alone must set it apart from most developing nations, though we now see similar contrasts in technology in India.

Local Energy Sources

Home-made methane has rapidly become an energy source for tens of millions of peasant families, allowing them to conserve coal, wood, straw and other things previously used for heating and cooking. Families are being taught to build single-unit airtight digesters which convert human and animal wastes, and crop residues into methane, or *biogas*.

The digester is a cylinder 2 metres deep and 3 metres across, with 40 mm thick concrete walls, which, in some places, are prefabricated slabs. Each is capped by a brick dome, sealed by clay, with a water covering, which prevents cracking and shows up leaks. The whole is sunk into a pit, and methane produced by the fermenting mass is led from the top, through a hose, to the house, where a valve regulates supplies and a meter checks the pressure. These are cheap to construct, for the labour can be supplied by the family and their neighbours.

The biogas burns cleanly and can be combusted in stoves, lamps, and rural industrial machinery, and in some places is used to generate electricity. Some villages construct larger tanks to provide energy for small electric generators.

113 Plant which can be locally installed to convert organic wastes to biogas and provide residues for use on the land.

The extraction of gas leaves a residue rich in nitrogen, phosphorus and other plant nutrients; and, because ammonia is not evaporated, this becomes a high quality fertiliser. Harmful parasites die during storage, so that the top of the residue can be siphoned off every week or two and safely sprayed on the crops. The sediment is usually removed twice a year, at planting times; it is stored with ammonia to make it quite harmless, and then mixed with the soil. In fact, methane production has improved sanitation and helped to prevent disease in rural areas, as well as efficiently using waste and saving other fuels.

Concave *solar reflectors* which concentrate the sun's energy have also been built by some rural communities, using steel, metal wire, mirrors, concrete and asphalt. Their angle has to be adjusted every twenty minutes or so; but, apart from this, after the cost of construction, there are no other expenses or labour. At the experimental stage these were restricted to selected 'solar villages'. They seem to be most suitable for southern China and the sunnier inland regions. However, solar energy is trapped by greenhouses and cloches, so that winter vegetables can be grown in the north. Solar heating through sunray panels is used for bathhouses, and also to heat insulated biogas converters during winter, when gas production falls with temperature — though

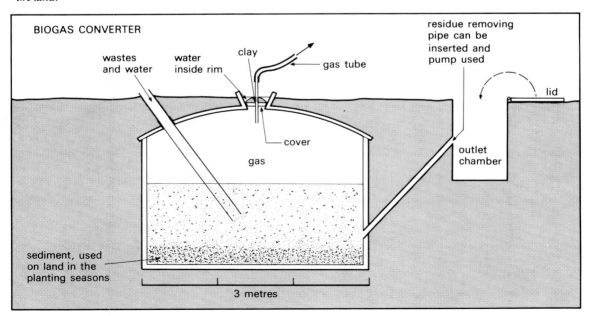

plastic sheeting is more generally used.

Tidal power has been experimented with; but, so far, the largest station, in Zhejiang province, only has a capacity of 3000 kw.

Geothermal energy is also being developed. The country around Fengshun, in the mountainous landscape inland of Shantou (Swatow) port, has numerous hot springs. At 800 m below the surface there is water at 102°C, and geothermal power stations have been constructed. A recent survey has shown two thousand possible sites in south-west China alone.

The development of these smaller, useful, but unconventional sources of energy is important to a country like China, with its large rural population. But, overall, China depends mostly on its coal resources, which are large enough for coal to figure prominently in its exports.

114 *Intensive cultivation, with the help of recycled organic matter, on the outskirts of Wuhan produces a variety of vegetables for the City markets. Here human and animal wastes and residues from the biodigester are carried to the fields in this typical 'honey cart' and transferred to wooden buckets.*

115 *Steelworks rise above factories and workers' flats in the north-western part of the heavy engineering city of Anshan, in Liaoning.*

Points to Consider

1 China has difficulties in developing its huge sources of energy: many are in remote areas; communications are still relatively poor; and modern plant is needed, even in existing coalfields.

2 There is particular value, in so large a country, in developing local energy sources, even when they are relatively small.

3 The policy of 'walking on two legs', like many of China's ways of tackling problems, is a response to years of under-development, national poverty and a huge, largely rural population.

4 The oilfield discoveries, and production and export of petroleum, have made a great difference to China's economy. But fossil fuels are wasting assets, and home demand will affect future oil exports.

5 Some parts of the country have hydro-electric potential but as yet few major developments.

6 The initial cost of hydro-electric development is formidable for a country like China, making joint ventures with foreign firms attractive.

7 Large hydro-electric developments are usually part of multi-purpose schemes, and in China the control of water for other purposes may be a priority.

8 The creation of biogas suits a rural population used to conserving any local materials likely to be of use.

9 The use of nuclear energy reflects the contrasting levels at which a developing country may operate – using high technology in some fields, but intermediate technology for the people as a whole.

5 Modern China: Mineral Wealth and Industrial Growth

Manufacturing Industries

China's industrial development is geared to improving technology at all levels. At the highest, China needs the trained technologists, research workers and equipment to develop nuclear power industries, launch its remote-sensing satellites, and work in its electronics industries. Joint projects involving foreign expertise, capital, and equipment are seen as mutually beneficial, and should eventually make China more independent in these fields if foreign confidence is maintained.

There have been abortive attempts to disperse China's iron and steel and heavy industries throughout the country; but these are most effectively developed close to sources of raw materials or manufactured components, and so tend to cluster about mineral deposits, ports, or large communications centres. Unfortunately, the distribution of products and parts for assembly industries is hampered by long distances and the still inadequate transportation facilities (p. 117).

The rising standards of living, with increasing consumer demands, are encouraging the proliferation of local factories and small workshops. However, some products, such as cotton textiles, which are important exports, are primarily manufactured in areas with raw materials and favourable transport facilities.

Most factories are state controlled, but increasing numbers are collectively owned. Various incentives now make for greater managerial efficiency. Part of the profits may now be re-invested by management, who have freedom to buy materials and parts, to compete with other industries, and hire skilled workers. Workers can gain through production bonuses, and in some cases have shares in the factory. Workers'

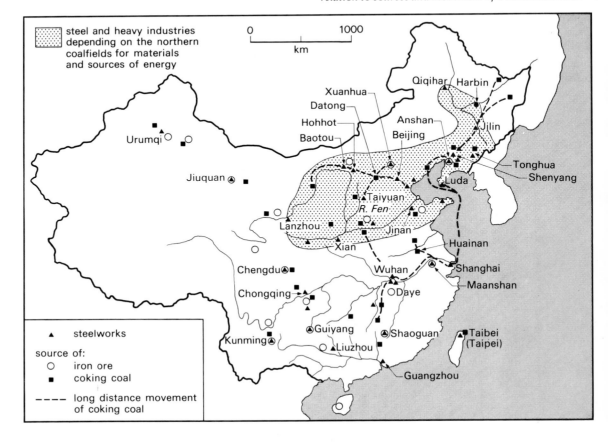

116 *The distribution of large-scale steel production in relation to sources and movement of iron ore and coal.*

committees now have more influence in working policies and practices.

Many large factories are social units, with housing, retail stores, schools, clinics, and welfare services. Workers' children may eventually be trained in that industry. Labour mobility is increasing, though still restricted compared with many countries.

Iron and Steel Industries

The north-eastern provinces, Manchuria, contain China's most important heavy industrial regions. Many of the steelworks and heavy industries built by Japan were destroyed at the end of the war, the Russians built iron and steel plants which helped China's reconstruction. But after 1960 it became more difficult to modernise the steelworks and establish other industries. Nevertheless, progress continued and the industrial cities expanded during the 'seventies. Now China is again using foreign expertise and equipment to install plant and introduce new technology.

At Anshan (Fig. 120) the rich iron ores, limestones and abundant coal supplies have led to a big output of iron and steel; Anshan's automated steel rolling mills and tubing plant are the country's chief source of steel in forms ready to be used for bridges, oil pipelines, and all kinds of machinery. Steelworks about Shenyang — at Fushun and Benxi (Penki), to the east at Tonghua (Tunghwa), and others further north, at Jilin (Kirin) help to make the north-east China's chief industrial region.

Shenyang, the capital of Liaoning province, is a major engineering city, sending machinery and machine tools to many parts of the country. Further north, Harbin's industries reflect its location as a route-centre in the heart of the plains: for it processes foods and manufactures agricultural machinery, from combine harvesters and tractors to small farm implements. It also turns out heavy machinery — pumps and turbines.

In northern China, other sources of iron ore supply nearby steel plants. Some send ores by rail to more distant steelworks. Thus mines at Xuanhua in northern Hubei feed local steelworks and send ore by rail to Beijing and to Taiyuan, in the Fen valley, both of which are supplied by coking coal from Datong. In Nei Mongol (Inner Mongolia), the steelworks at Baotou use local ores and limestone, and also obtain coal from Datong, and from mines to the south-west. For similar reasons, Hohhot, the regional capital, established steelworks.

In central China Wuhan is an important route-centre. Situated where the Han river joins the Chang jiang, it is really three closely linked towns — Wuchang, Hankou and Hanyang (Fig. 124). Hanyang has had a steel industry for a long time; but soon after the Chang jiang was bridged (in 1957) a huge iron and steel complex was built about 8 km down-river from Wuchang, and this now has a large steel-rolling mill. Iron ore and limestone are brought, by an electrified railway, from Daye about 65 kms to the south-east. Before this, Daye sent its ore to a port on the Chang jiang, where an iron and steel works helped to turn nearby Huangshi into an industrial town. The extra power demands of the new steel mills at Wuhan left this region short of energy, until electricity from the Gezhou projects provided power for its growing industries.

Much further down the Chang jiang, iron ore is mined at Maanshan, just to the west of the river, in Anhui province (Fig. 116). Here an old iron and steel works has developed into a large integrated plant, which helps to supply industries in Shanghai.

In Shanghai, steel production has been based on water-borne raw materials, brought by river and by sea. Today its integrated steelworks, which turn out steel alloys and electroplated metals, still receives many raw and semi-processed materials by ship down the Chang jiang. Coal also comes by sea from the northern coalports.

In southern China, most of the steelworks are not on this scale. Liuzhou has a medium-size complex which receives ores from the Xi basin to the south, and Guiyang's steel production is based on local ores. The considerable reserves of iron ore near the west coast of Hainan island will be exploited as it is developed industrially as a special economic area.

In western central China, Sichuan has large reserves of iron ore, and steelworks near Chengdu use local coking coal. Iron ore and coal are also mined south of Chongqing, whose steel industry has been enlarged and modernised.

In the southwest, on the Yunnan plateau, Kunming's steelworks benefit from coal, iron ore and limestone within 40 km of the city. Transport costs for bulky materials are high, so there is a great advantage in producing iron and steel in these rapidly developing western regions.

The dry north-west benefits similarly from the huge deposits of rich iron ore in western Gansu province. An integrated iron and steel works has been built at Jiuquan, 80 km east of Yumen. Even further west, iron ores and coal deposits north of the Tian Shan supply steelworks at Urumqi (Fig. 116) and feed smaller plants further north.

It is worth noting that though many of the big steel-producing towns are located close to iron ore mines, some large cities find it an advantage to produce steel locally, despite the cost of bringing raw materials a considerable distance: as in the case of Shanghai, served by water transport, and of Xian and Lanzhou, which are supplied by rail.

Non Ferrous Minerals

Many other metals are needed to produce steel of particular quality, and China is fortunate in having most of them in quantity. Tungsten and antimony ores are so abundant that, despite China's own increasing demands, they are valuable exports. Manganese, molybdenum and nickel are also plentiful; and there are great reserves of rare earth elements.

There are numerous sources of non-ferrous metals – copper, zinc, lead, tin, silver, mercury and aluminium – and graphite also occurs in quantity. The prospects for further finds are good, for much of this large country awaits detailed mineral exploration.

117 Geological processes concentrate non-ferrous metals in certain areas. In each of the shaded zones, and those shown by lettering, there are productive mines.

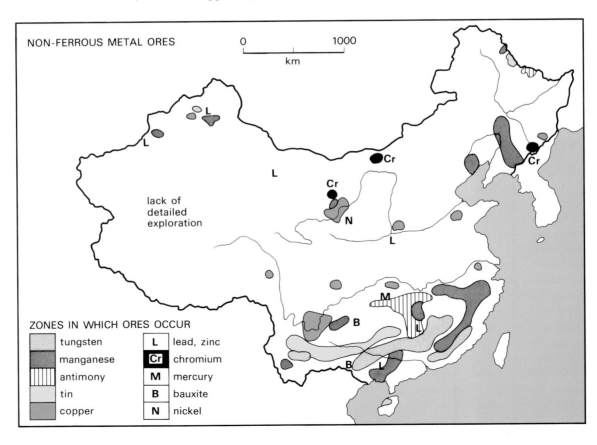

118 *A Beijing factory manufactures electro-magnetic equipment. China's industrial cities now produce most of the country's generating plant, and are introducing advanced technology, especially in the electronics field.*

A high proportion of these minerals comes from the rocks of southern China. Metals mined near the Heilong (Amur) river are primarily used in the industries in the north-east; and China is already exploiting the many potentially rich regions in the far west.

Not all the reserves are abundant. China's output of zinc, copper and lead are, as yet, only moderate, in relation to the country's present and future needs.

Salt is used in chemical industries, as well as for domestic purposes. Along the coasts, it is produced by sea-water evaporation. In Sichuan deep deposits in rock strata are obtained both by mining and from brine wells. Far inland, huge accumulations lie in old lake beds.

The Large Industrial Centres

We have seen that heavy industries are often concentrated where suitable raw materials coincide, especially those based on iron ore and coal. Petroleum refining and petrochemical industries are developed at the oilfields; though oil may be pumped long distances to refineries and chemical works. The latter may be the source of other industries: at Wuhan their polyester supplies textile factories (Fig. 130)

Many cities use local and regional produce in their manufacturing industries. Thus cotton from the Chang jiang's lower plains and delta lands supplies textile mills at Shanghai. Cotton from the Wei valley goes to Xian; and irrigated cotton fields in western Xinjiang feed Urumqi's factories. The textile factories in Xian and Urumqi also receive wool from the north-western grazing lands.

Most large cities have a variety of industries which serve their own population and the nearby rural areas — though they may come to supply a wider market. This applies especially to the city-ports where industries use imported raw materials. Their factories also assemble mechanical products, using machinery, metal parts and materials delivered from other parts of China, or now imported, once more, from foreign countries. The present policy is to make as many

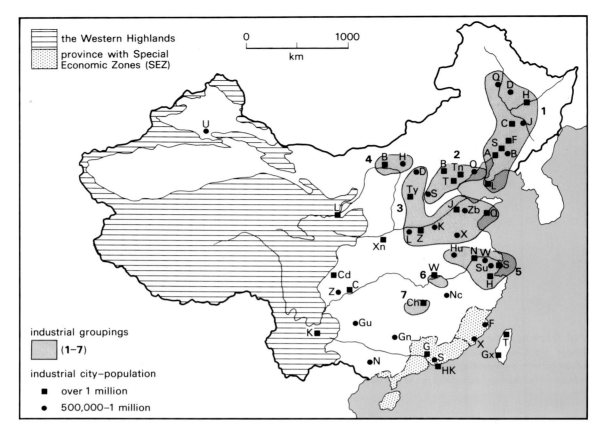

the Western Highlands
province with Special
Economic Zones (SEZ)

0   1000
km

industrial groupings

(1–7)

industrial city-population

■ over 1 million

● 500,000–1 million

119 *The initials indicate the large industrial cities named in the text; many of them are grouped (1–7) to bring out common advantages of location, materials and energy sources.*

of the industrial components as possible in China itself; but in order to establish Chinese industries as quickly as possible, plant and materials may be brought in from overseas.

The diversity of industries in large Chinese cities is shown by those in Tianjin (Tientsin), which include iron and steel, heavy machinery and vehicles, chemicals, electronic goods, watches, sewing machines, carpets, cameras, and a wide range of daily consumer goods for its eight million people (p. 134). In the same way, Shanghai's industries range from steel, ship-building, heavy machinery, chemicals, fertilisers, textiles, TVs, and precision instruments to those making bicycles, radios, clocks, light bulbs, vacuum flasks, household fittings, prepared foods, sweets and other commodities needed by millions of families. Those of the river port Nanjing (Nanking) include metallurgy, oil refining,

manufacturing machine tools, telecommunication equipment, optical instruments, synthetic fibres and processed foods; while over a thousand other state, collective, and individual enterprises serve its three million consumers and nearby rural areas of the Chang jiang plainlands.

The Distribution of Industrial Cities

Fig. 119 shows how the major industrial centres are grouped in various parts of China. Cities in these groupings tend to have industries in common; but some have specialist activities associated with a port, or rural regional centre, or nearby raw materials. It also shows individual regional cities, such as Lanzhou and Kunming, which have a wide range of industries. Special Economic Zones and designated ports have been set up for joint foreign/Chinese developments aimed at encouraging investment in modern industries. (p. 111).

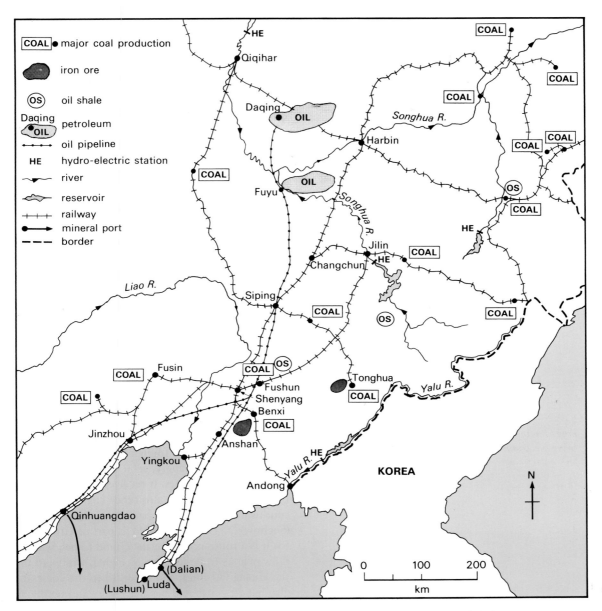

120 *Energy sources, manufacturing centres and ports of China's industrially important north-east.*

There are numerous larger thermal power stations and apart from the major hydro-electric stations, hundreds of smaller ones.

The names may be unfamiliar but grouping helps to explain the location of many of these centres, which are so important to China's economy and modernisation programme.

The Northern Industrial Groups

Group 1 Here many of the industrial cities are based on the coal, iron ore and petroleum resources of the north-east. They include Shenyang (S), Anshan (A), Fushun (F), Benxi (Penki) (B), Changchun (C), Jilin (Kirin) (J), Harbin (H), Qiqihar (Tsitsihar) (Q), Daqing (Taching) (D), and the industrial port complex called Luda (L), made up of the ports of Lushun and Dalian, which serves this mineral-rich north-eastern region and has large shipyards.

Group 2 takes in the cities of Beijing (Peking), Tianjin (Tientsin) and Tangshan, situated on the lowlands to the west of the Gulf of Bohai. Beijing (B) and Tianjin (T), described on pp. 131–4, have a whole range of industries, from iron and steel, heavy engineering, petro-chemicals, vehicles, agricultural equipment and electronic goods to a host of small consumer goods for sale in the stores. Tangshan (Tn) also produces steel and machinery and has oil refining and textile industries. It is recovering, like Tianjin, from a disastrous earthquake in 1976.

In a sense, these cities belong to those in Group 3, which rely on the northern coalfields for energy and for the coke used in steel-making; Qinhuangdao (Chinwangtao) (Q) is a major coal-exporting port. The metal and textile city of Shijiazhuang (S), which is on the railway south from Beijing, may be seen as a link between Groups 2 and 3.

Group 3 includes a wide variety of industrial towns on, or close to coal-mining areas; for the coalfields which run southwards from Datong are also exposed to the west of the Shandong peninsula.

121 Lowry-like figures in the snowy street, and crossing basket ball pitches in the factory compound, add to the image of Taiyuan described in Fig. 122.

Datong (D), a main coal mining and distributing industrial centre, just south of the Great Wall manufactures locomotives. A railway runs south to Taiyuan (Ty), in a fertile basin with a long history of settlement. Its very large iron ore and coal deposits are mined locally. Its factories dominate the city of a million people, and produce textiles, steel, and chemicals. Smaller mining towns lie close to the river Fen and in the hills to the east. The railway which runs down this closely farmed valley crosses the Huang He and then branches, west to Xian and east towards Luoyang (L). The latter lies on a tributary to the Huang He in a rich agricultural countryside, and was once the capital of ancient China. It is now an industrial city which makes mining equipment, pumps, tractors, ball bearings and glass. Like the other industrial cities Zengzhou (Chengchow) (Z) and Kaifeng (K) further down the Huang He valley, it benefits from energy generated at the Sanmen dam (p. 96).

Further east Jinan (J), the capital of Shandong, lies just south of the river. It is another coal-mining city close to iron ore deposits, yet part of an agricultural countryside, with flour mills as well as steelworks and chemical and metallurgical factories. A railway runs to the major sea-port, air-port, and resort of Qingdao (Q) whose factories benefit from foreign investments and produce steel, machinery, vehicles, TV equipment, and textiles. It receives coal by rail from Zibo (Zb), which also sends coal southwards to the Chang jiang ports. Xuzhou (Suchow) (X) can be regarded as part of Group 3, for it is a route-centre on the Grand Canal, with railway links to Beijing and Shanghai, westward to the Huang He cities, and eastward to the coast. It also handles coal, and has machinery and textile industries.

The iron and steel cities in **Group 4** are only shown separately because of their location in the great northern grasslands of Nei Mongol (Inner Mongolia): for they, too, obtain coal from mines in Shanxi. The iron and steel complex at Baotou (Paotow) (B) is a very large one, and was only completed in the 1960s; and that at Hohhot (H), the regional capital and woollen manufacturing city, was established even more recently.

Fig. 119 helps to locate each of these large towns. Even so, it is difficult at first to think of

them as lively, active cities, serving a closely populated countryside about them, in which other lesser, but large market towns are also bustling centres of activity with small factories boosted by the recent surge in consumerism. The lists of industries give some idea of their economic importance, and it is instructive to notice how they are grouped in relation to energy resources, mineral deposits, and water routes, and to the densely populated parts of rural China.

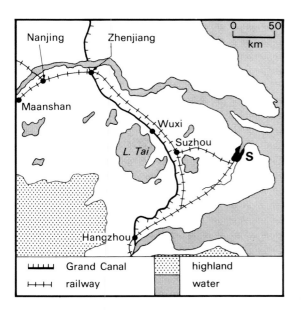

122 Taiyuan, with its textile mills under winter snow, lies in the Fen valley, which has large coal and iron ore deposits.

Industrial Groups in Central China

Group 5 includes the cities of the lower Chang jiang and its delta lands. The huge city-port, Shanghai (S), is described on pp. 135–6. With its outer districts, it covers more than 6000 km², and in this area live some twelve million people. There are also other large industrial cities in this densely populated part of China, each with over a million inhabitants. The region is well served by waterways and railways. Shanghai, for instance, receives raw materials and manufactured goods from towns on the rivers and canals, as well as from ocean-going and coastal vessels.

A number of these now multi-industrial cities have long been known for silk production. Hangzhou (Hangchow) (H), at the southern end of the Grand Canal, has long been famed for its silk. The industry remains, but there are now steelworks, oil refineries, petro-chemical works, and electronics industries; and, appropriately, for a city serving a rich agricultural countryside, it produces light tractors and trucks. Further north, Suzhou (Soochow) (Su) on the Grand Canal, was

123 The Grand Canal and cities on the major waterways. (S – Shanghai).

also renowned for its silk and still produces high quality textiles. But it now specialises in metallurgy, precision instruments, machine tools and electronic products, and has large chemical works. Suzhou, too, serves the rural population, and barges bring agricultural produce to its processing factories. It is linked by canal to Wuxi (Wuhsi) (W), on Lake Tai. This is another old silk city, now noted for high technology products – machine tools and precision instruments – and craftware in enamels and glass. It has other light industries, and turns out large numbers of bicycles.

Nanjing (Nanking) (N), the former capital city, lies 300 km north-west of Shanghai. As a large river port and route centre on the Chang jiang, its importance has grown since the river bridge was opened in 1968, linking Shanghai directly by road and rail with Beijing. Nanjing is the largest inland port and handles ocean-going freighters. It tranships coal and the products of its refineries to other parts of central and southern China. Its industries are described on p. 106.

Huainan (Hu) is included in Group 5, for as a coalfield manufacturing town it is important to the industrial growth of this part of China. Its coal reaches power stations and industries along the Chang jiang via the railways and river ports.

Wuhan is a conurbation: as a triple city with nearby industrial towns, it is shown as **Group 6**. It is a river port and route-centre in the same category as Nanjing (Fig. 124). Some four million people live in these moist lowlands about the confluence of the Han jiang and Chang jiang, protected from flooding by a series of reinforced dykes. Hanyang and Hankow are, respectively, on the right and left banks of the Han, with Wuchang across on the right bank of the Chang jiang. Its big iron and steel complex is further downstream.

124 Wuhan, with its heavy industries, located at the convergence of natural routeways on the Chang jiang lowlands.

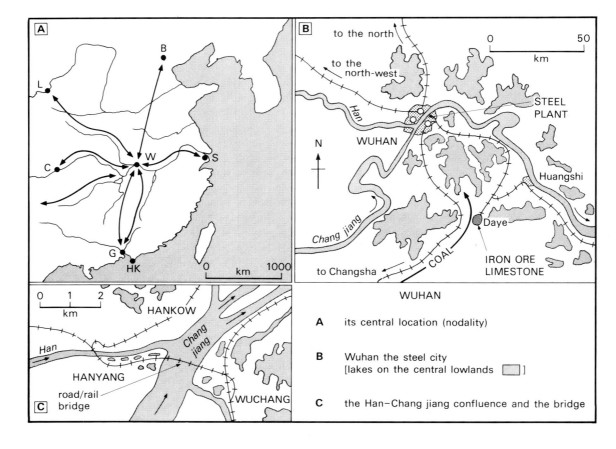

WUHAN

A   its central location (nodality)

B   Wuhan the steel city
[lakes on the central lowlands ▨]

C   the Han–Chang jiang confluence and the bridge

125 A steelworks in Wuhan which depends on rail transport for its materials.

Wuhan's real asset, as a major industrial city, is its natural location as a route centre. As a port, it can take ships up to 15 000 tonnes during the high-water summer months; but only up to 5000 tonnes for the rest of the year. Like, Nanjing, it has benefited greatly from the bridging of the Chang jiang. It is not just a steel city, but has factories producing chemicals, fertilisers, textiles and many light engineering products. Production has been hampered by power shortages, but now energy comes from the Gezhou project and via power lines from the north.

Further south is Changsha (Ch), the capital of Hunan. This is a province with surplus rice, and the city has many grain mills. Being a port on the river Xiang, it has a wide hinterland, and barges still arrive with grain, timber and coal; though today railways serve what is a mineral-rich area. Changsha is really the largest centre of a three-city industrial region, **Group 7**. In the nearby towns, factories smelt lead and zinc, and steelworks use local manganese; Changsha itself produces aluminium, using hydro-electric energy, and turns out machine tools and precision instruments.

The Special Economic Zones

China has been concentrating particularly on the industrial development of ports and the areas immediately about them.

Today, 14 ports and the island province of Hainan have been designated open economic development zones, where, with tax incentives for foreign investors, modern industries are encouraged. Besides these, there are Special Economic Zones (SEZs) in Fujiang and Guangdong provinces, encouraging foreign investment, foreign firms, and joint ventures, manufacturing goods from foreign materials and components, as well as from Chinese ones. Foreign expertise is harnessed, especially in enterprises requiring much capital and using high technology. These aim to bring in foreign currency, but also to manufacture advanced products for the home market. They also gain by experiencing and adopting new management and production techniques. There are special incentives, such as tax advantages on profits from industries within these zones.

However, the internal political struggles of 1989 may have drastic consequences should they cause foreign investments to dry up.

In Guangdong, where Guangzhou already has

special facilities for foreign investors, Shenzhen has rapidly been developed in a Special Economic Zone near the Hong Kong border; in a few years it has become a planned city with over half a million people. There are joint ventures with foreign firms, especially from Hong Kong, Japan and the USA, and investments in a wide range of high-tech industries involving electronics, and also in printing, textiles, and vehicle assembly. The Development Corporation cleared the land and provided roads, electricity, water, sewerage, and recreation facilities.

Shenzhen SEZ is served by a new port. Skilled workers and their families have been brought in from many parts of China, and wages and housing facilities are well above the national average. It has close economic connections with Hong Kong, whose territory it adjoins, and which will eventually become a Special Administrative Region of China. The nuclear power station at Daya Bay boosts the electricity supply for the whole developing industrial area. There are now tourist facilities. Tourism is also a joint venture between Guangdong's other SEZ, at Zhuhai, and Macao, across its border (p. 137).

Another Special Economic Zone lies about Xiamen (Amoy) (X), an island linked to a bay on the Fujian coast. Its new port, Dongdu, is well placed for trade with Hong Kong, Taiwan, and south-east Asian ports. It is well served by roads and railways and has a large airport. Its industries include electronics equipment, photographic and TV manufactures; and its university and scientific research institutes work on new technologies.

Further south, Shantou SEZ, about the Han estuary, includes a container port. Many Chinese have returned from abroad and helped it create overseas trade.

Regional Industrial Centres

The other large cities shown in Fig. 119 are regional industrial centres of great local importance; most are provincial capitals. Nanchang (Nc), for example, is the capital of Jianxi province. It is another waterway town, strengthened by railway links, and, like Changsha, combines agricultural industries – cotton mills,

126 A girl tending a plant in a heavy machine-tools factory in Kunming. A third of the workers are women.

rice mills and vegetable oil factories – with machine manufacturing, and vehicle and aircraft production.

Nanning (N) and Guiyang (Kweiyang) (Gu) are, respectively, regional and provincial capitals. In the case of Guiyang, local minerals – coal, mercury, manganese and bauxite (aluminium ore) – have helped to make it a metal manufacturing city, with steelworks and heavy industries.

Guilin (Kweilin) (Gn) is shown, for its chief livelihood is related to the striking scenery of the steep-sided hills of karst limestone – tourism. The tourist industry earns foreign currency and so is an important one for China. Guilin's airport has been improved to cope with the influx of tourists.

Further west, Kunming (K) lies in a basin on the Yunnan plateau, beside Lake Dian Chi. Its role as a regional centre is described on p. 139. Its steelworks are based on local raw materials, and it manufactures trucks, tools and electrical equipment (copper is produced in Yunnan). It also has many small factories making consumer goods, for its population is more than a million.

Chongqing (Chungking) (C) lies where the Jialing river meets the Chang jiang in the south of the Sichuan basin. The city rises up the steep

127 *The centre of Shenzhen, where new offices and banks, the advertisements and traffic point to the rapid industrial – commercial development in this Special Economic Zone.*

wedge of land between the rivers. During the Japanese war, industrial plant was brought here from the east. Today, with a population of over four million, it is expanding with the development of Sichuan's agricultural, mineral and energy resources. Steel industries enable it to manufacture equipment and plant for thousands of factories, including joint-foreign enterprises, such as motorcycle production. The bridging of the Jialing and Chang jiang, navigational improvements, and energy generated near Yichang, make this route-centre increasingly important industrially.

Sichuan's capital, Chengdu (Cd), is an old settlement on a very rich agricultural plain (p. 72) with a number of satellite manufacturing towns nearby. Nearly four million people live in the city, suburbs and immediate surroundings. Coal and natural gas are invaluable sources of energy for a city so far inland; so, besides its traditional silk industry, it has many forms of engineering, and produces computers and other electronic apparatus. It refines aluminium, has metallurgical industries, and makes fertilisers and other chemicals.

Chengdu and Chongqing are by no means the only industrial centres in Sichuan. The country's most populous province is a rapidly developing part of China. Many of the towns on the plains about Chengdu, and others near the railway to Chongqing, are acquiring modern industries. Zigong (Tzukung) (Z), Sichuan's third city has a major chemical complex.

Away to the north, the growing industrial city Xian (Sian) (X) in the Wei valley could also be regarded as part of Group 3, with its rail links to the northern coalfields and energy from the Sanmen dam. But this city, of two million people, is primarily a regional centre in a rich valley amid the loess lands. The modern successor of ancient Chang-an, Xian is now the capital of Shaanxi province. It has steelworks and engineering industries. Many of its industries are associated with agriculture — manufacturing textiles and fertilisers — , and it makes machine tools, electric engines and pumps for use in rural areas.

128 *Flats for workers within the machine-tools factory (Fig. 126). There are also schools, a small hospital (Fig. 129), and some farmland.*

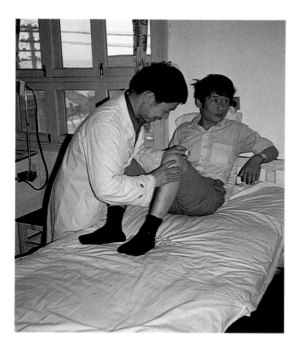

129 *A worker with a knee injury being treated by acupuncture in the factory hospital.*

Lanzhou (Lanchow) (L), the capital of Gansu province, is situated on the upper reaches of the Huang He, and electricity from the great dam up-river (p. 96) has greatly added to its industrial potential. It processes aluminium and copper, is a centre of the nuclear energy industry, and has important oil refineries and petro-chemical works (p. 93) and other large industries, which include machine manufacturing and woollen mills. Lanzhou's old town, for so long a route-centre for the dry north-west, lies apart from the modern manufacturing areas.

Finally, we look at Urumqi (Urumchi) (U) and the far western interior (p. 85), where the transfer of so many Han Chinese to Xinjiang provided a skilled workforce. The city, supplied by the irrigated farmlands about it, draws on the recently developed mineral resources to produce its steel, oil products and chemicals. It now manufacturers tractors and farm machinery, and its factories receive and process commercial crops, notably cotton and sugar cane. The completion of the road and rail routes linking Urumqi to the east (p. 123) speeded up its development.

Fig. 119 also shows the industrial city-ports of Hong Kong (HK) (p. 152) and Gaoxiong (Gx) in Taiwan (p. 162). These, like Taibei (T), the Taiwanese capital, have many light industries which compete in world markets, including textiles and electronics; and each is now developing heavier industries.

By separating these large cities into groups and regional centres, we can focus on particular parts of mainland China where manufacturing industries are well developed. But there are many other, smaller towns within these groups, and scattered over the provinces, where numerous people are employed in large-scale manufacturing: and, of course, there are the engineers, machine operators, carpenters and other skilled men and women employed in factories and workshops set up in small towns all over the country.

Manufacturing For, and By, the Rural Population

Factories in the large industrial regions supply many of the products used in the countryside. Fertilisers come from petro-chemical works in Sichuan and the north-eastern oilfields; engines and pumps from the steel cities of Anshan and Wuhan; tractors are distributed from factories in Harbin, Shanghai, and Luoyang. But many of these agricultural inputs are now manufactured regionally. A considerable proportion of the light rural machinery, pumps and implements now come from small factories at county level and below. Much of the cement is produced in small works, and brick-making, as always, is a widespread rural industry. Half of China's chemical fertiliser has come from small factories; though fewer, larger regional plants appear more suitable economically.

The dispersal of industry eases problems caused by poor communications and the great distances involved; for there are transport bottlenecks despite the drive to extend and improve communications throughout China. It has been a key policy to encourage townships to set up small factories to process local vegetable and animal produce and prepare canned fruits, soya bean products, vegetable oils, fibres and leathergoods, or whatever commodities are related to the regional agriculture. This keeps down the costs to the local people and leads to more widespread industrial employment. A proportion of a crop may be processed locally, and the rest, perhaps the bulk of it, sent to larger factories elsewhere. Thus there are numerous small cotton mills in each of the growing regions which supply the textile industries in Shanghai, Wuhan and Tianjin. Grain milling has also become a regional industry, whereas, once, most of the flour came from large mills in big cities or in ports which received wheat imports.

130 A textile factory started by a collective in Wuhan uses polyester from local chemical works. Three tax-free years enabled them to invest in equipment and increase production eight-fold during that period.

131 Wide areas covered by transparent plastic sheets produce vegetables between Xian's old city wall and the industrial district beyond. Such thick earthen walls, faced with brick, once surrounded most northern towns and cities.

132 *Girls making cloisonnée (enamel ware) articles in a Luoyang factory. Much craftwork is exported, especially through Hong Kong.*

Craft Industries

Individual craft workers, producing fine articles in metals, stone, clay, wood, bamboo, or textiles have always been found throughout the country. In all periods, master craftsmen have used skill and resourcefulness to fashion high quality, artistic artifacts.

Talent is still recognised, and many men and women find scope for skill and inventiveness in local communities. Others work in small factories, especially in the cities, where there are handicraft centres at which apprentices can learn design, construction and techniques from master craftsmen. Certain cities have acquired, and retain, a reputation for a particular craft – Changsha for embroidery and lacquerwork, Suzhou for jade, Nanjing for ceramics, and so on. But apart from craft workshops in large cities, there are thousands of smaller centres where people are encouraged to work in local, regional styles in various materials.

Points to Consider

1 It would help if manufacturing industries were spread more widely, but parts of China are particularly well suited to develop heavy industries.
2 The location of China's sources of coal and iron ore have made railway construction and improvements of prime importance. Railway bottlenecks have hampered manufacturing productivity in a number of areas.
3 Riverside and coastal locations for steelworks have particular advantages, but their location must be related to where there is adequate demand for the products.
4 The grouping of large industrial cities is related to various facts – the presence of energy sources; local raw materials; other industries which need the products; a well-populated region; an advantageous transport route. Cities within each group shown in Fig. 119 share many of these advantages, but may also have much in common with those in adjacent groups.
5 The demands of a large local population are reflected by the many different kinds of industries in the big cities.
6 China tries to industrialise quickly, which can lead to planning errors. Wuhan's steel rolling mill (from West Germany) was once unable to operate without overloading local electricity sources. Shanghai's great steelworks (with Japanese plant) was sited on moving sands, which concrete injection failed, at first, to secure.
7 Overmanning has impaired the efficiency of many Chinese factories, providing token jobs for those who would otherwise be unemployed. Modern plant needing a trimmed down workforce can create social problems.
8 Collectively-owned factories, responsible for their own profits and losses after contribution to the state, now use profits to develop new types of product, compete with others, and choose their workforce.

6 Modern China: Improving the Communications

Transport over the Ages

For thousands of years communications and transport changed little. Draught animals and people on foot moved along dirt tracks. In the loess lands cart wheels wore deep into the loose material and roads were often sunk below the level of the countryside – an advantage in the bitter winter months. In the southern hill country, the roads were more often rocky tracks, though the more important sections were paved. Along these people carried loads balanced on either side of their shoulder poles, or pushed materials in their wheelbarrows. Vast distances and difficult terrain made land transport a slow process.

The Waterways

For these reasons, water transport has been of particular importance through the ages. In the north, where low water in the winter months affects navigation, people relied to a great extent on transport by horses, mules and donkeys; Bactrian (two-humped) camels carried loads across the western deserts. Nevertheless, there was busy traffic wherever a river or canal could act as a waterway, especially in eastern China and the Sichuan basin. In southern and central China, and

133 Long-distance locomotives, like that shown on p. 117, play a great part in developing a country as large as China.

in the delta lands, the navigable streams, rivers and lakes were linked by numerous canals, and water transport was, and still is of great importance. At the same time, animal transport was also used, especially in the uplands; narrow carts drawn by several small horses are still a feature in the hill country of the south-west.

The general flow of the main rivers has given communications an east–west trend. Efforts were made to link the main river systems even before the first canal connecting the Chang jiang and Huang He was dug (p. 36). Some remarkable feats of engineering provided a north–south link between the Xi and Chang jiang as early as 215 BC, through a canal connecting their tributaries, the Gui and Xiang rivers.

In modern times, the great rivers flowing eastwards and their frequent flooding have hampered long-distance road and rail communications between north and south. It is difficult and expensive to bridge such wide rivers, with their fluctuating levels, but we have seen the great value of the long road and rail bridges across the Chang jiang at Wuhan and Nanjing.

The Chang jiang and its tributaries have always carried more traffic by far than the other rivers. Junks have served the many large and small river ports over the ages. Above Yichang, however, the river cascades through the gorges and boats had to be hauled up-river by teams of men, toiling up paths cut into the sides of the gorge; even then progress was hazardous. Later, dredging and rock clearing allowed small, powered craft to pass through the gorges. Now, at the Gezhou dam (p. 97) ships can be lifted by hoists and continue up-stream towards Chongqing, and there are plans for new dams in the gorges to create even greater depths up-river.

Down-river, the Europeans established regular freight trade through the *treaty ports*. Today, the large river ports have well-organised docks, capable of dealing with a variety of cargoes. The role of Nanjing as a river port is described on p. 110; and further down-stream another busy river port, Zhenjiang, is located where the Grand Canal reaches the Chang jiang from the south.

134 Horse transport is still widely used and, as with handcarts, good wheels and tyres make for efficiency.

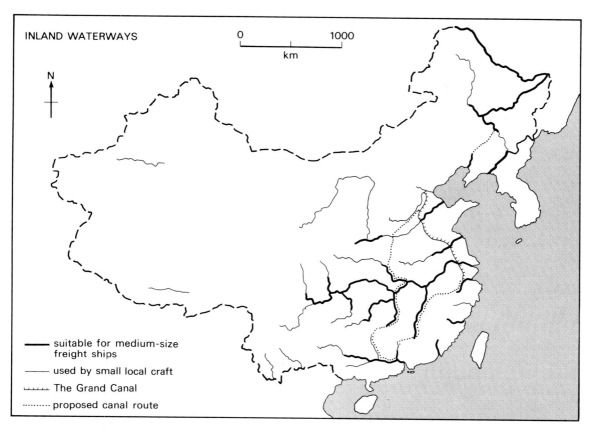

INLAND WATERWAYS

0   1000

km

N

— suitable for medium-size freight ships

— used by small local craft

⊢⊢⊢ The Grand Canal

.... proposed canal route

135 Navigable waterways and proposals for new, linking routes.

136 Sacks being pulled up a ramp on the steep banks of the Chang jiang into a Chongqing warehouse.

There are seasonal restrictions on the size of
shipping, however, and the industrial areas about
Wuhan can be served by vessels drawing not more
than 2 m in the winter low-water period,
compared with 9 m draught in summer. But most
of the river traffic is still made up of small craft,
which together transport a large quantity of goods
between the towns and villages; this is also true of
craft using the tributary rivers.

In the south, the Xi jiang carries much river
traffic. Guangzhou (Canton), with its deep-water
port, Huangpu, serves ocean-going vessels using
the Pearl river estuary, and it is a focal point for
the exchange of goods, for river trade extends far
inland. Vessels of 2000 tonnes can reach Wuzhou
(Wuchow), and, here too, smaller craft make great
use of the tributaries.

It is proposed to develop linking waterways
which will carry inland shipping from
Guangzhou right through to Beijing. Fig. 135
shows the suggested routes: a western one for
southward traffic and an eastern one for north-

137 *Long-boats pass through a lock between the
Grand Canal and the Chang jiang, at Yangzhou.*
138 *Water transport is widely used, wherever possible.
This ship, with patched sails, carries a heavy cargo of
rocks across Lake Dian Chi.*

139 Long-distance trucks carry pipes from Xian and a local tractor hauls timber along a well-surfaced road in Lintong. Women use a hot spring to wash clothes. Notice, again, the intensive vegetable growing.

bound vessels. Notice the part that the Grand Canal would continue to play in such a project. The scheme would, of course, involve lock building as well as canal extensions; but this is by no means impossible, and, in view of traffic on existing sections, seems desirable.

In north-east China, the Songhua river carries timber, grain and passenger traffic. Plans have been made to build a canal joining the Amur river to the Yellow Sea, and to extend this to link the Songhua river with the Liao, near Changchun. In winter, of course, the freezing conditions in the north, prevents water transport for long periods.

The Roads

The state helps local townships improve and extend the main road links between important regional towns. Generally, the townships are responsible for the lesser country roads, which give smaller villages better access to local markets, and make the collection and distribution of goods more efficient, even though they are sometimes just improved dry weather tracks. They help to maintain communications from county and township levels down to the local villages. The central government is responsible for building long

140 Light tractors, like this one returning from an urban market, have low fuel consumption and are used in most parts of rural China.

trunk roads, and bridge building has been given priority to help extend the highway system.

Many more road vehicles are now used in the rural areas, and increasing numbers of official cars, trucks and taxis in the cities; where there is generally good, if overcrowded, public transport, with coaches and/or trolley buses running in the main streets of the large cities. Trucks and trailers thread through city streets thronged with bicycles, and noisy with the incessant purping of horns. There are now some privately owned taxis, and a small but growing number of private cars.

141 China's railway system has expanded to serve a much larger number of rural settlements and has helped to support development in remote areas. Many improvements are still needed in this vast network.

The Railways

The railways are immensely important for carrying both freight and passengers. They link the major regions and the big cities, and stimulate settlement and industrial development in the more remote parts of the country. Fig. 141 shows what great progress has been made in extending China's railway systems and creating a denser network, despite the post-war need to re-lay tracks and rebuild bridges and despite the setbacks to the economy described on p. 46. Nevertheless there is a continuing need for extension and improvements. Investment is being made to double-track or electrify key lines to industrial regions. In its programme for modernisation the government must decide priorities for investment. Unless the railways are efficient,

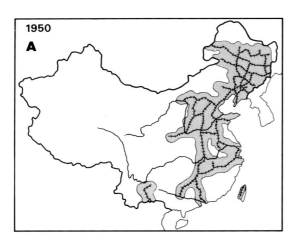

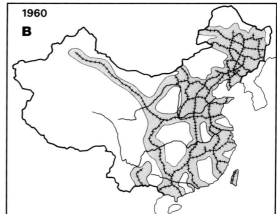

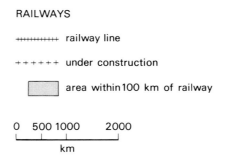

RAILWAYS

++++++++ railway line

+ + + + + + under construction

▨ area within 100 km of railway

0 500 1000   2000
└──┴──┴─────────┘
         km

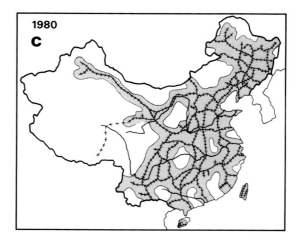

142 *A long steam-powered passenger train passes through the Langshan ranges north of Beijing, on its way to Baotou.*

they hamper industrial progress, despite the installation of modern plant in the factories.

The railways seen in Fig. 141A were mostly built with foreign capital. They served the ports of Guangzhou (Canton), linked to Kowloon on Hong Kong's mainland, Shanghai, Qingdao, Tianjin, and Luda (Dalian). In the economically important north-east (Manchuria) the railway network was largely built by the USSR and Japan. Notice the lack of railways in western China, the isolation of Kunming, and the gap to the east of Wuhan. The north—south rail links were not complete, for trains had to be ferried across the Chang jiang (Yangtze) until the river was bridged, first at Wuhan in 1951, then at Chongqing in 1959, and at Nanjing in 1969.

Not only were new rail routes needed, but double tracks had to be laid between the more important centres, and existing lines had to be maintained, often in very difficult country. Fig. 141B shows that by 1960 there was a more complete network, with links between provincial capitals in the west; and a line had just been extended to the far west of Xinjiang (Sinkiang).

By 1980 (Fig. 141C) the eastern and central lines formed a much closer network. One of those under construction follows a high route across Tibet to Lhasa. But although Wuhan is now connected by a branch line to the Beijing—

Shanghai railway, it says much for the use of the Chang jiang as a waterway that there is still no direct line connecting Wuhan to the delta lands.

Some stretches of railway are now electrified: this helps in difficult terrain, where steam engines find the going difficult: a number of high-gradient lines in Sichuan are electrified. Diesels are now produced at locomotive works in Datong and Luda.

143 *Railways serve more and more of the rural population (Fig. 141). Many country platforms are short: here at Ebian, in western Sichuan, passengers run to their allocated compartment.*

Air Transport

Beijing, Shanghai and Guangzhou have large international airports, and internal air transport has much increased in recent years. CAAC, the Chinese airline, operates jets and propeller aircraft on routes which serve scores of Chinese cities and many smaller route centres and tourist places, like Guilin. There are scheduled services, much used by officials, PLA members, and technicians of various kinds. These are an increasing advantage for rapid communication; but land and water transport carry the bulk of China's goods and travellers.

144 *Members of a PLA workforce and local officials wait to board a plane at Simao, a regional centre in the far south-west (Fig. 86).*

145 *Beyond the moat and the curving roofs of the Forbidden City rise the modern buildings of central Beijing.*

Points to Consider

1 China's physical structure has much to do with the west–east courses of the great rivers, and the need to build north-south linking canals.

2 The same applies to the north–south linking railways, though these have been hampered by the rivers themselves.

3 Canal building is still being extended and old canals widened and deepened, for movement by water is a cheap form of bulk transport.

4 China relies mainly on railways for long-distance movements, rather than waterways and roads.

5 Fig. 141 shows that the railway network has been extended and made more complex, but it cannot show other important requirements – the need for more double-tracking, electrification, and new stock; which together are a further drain on China's investment capital.

6 The close network of railways in the north-east was established in the early twentieth century, and correctly points to the economic importance of the region.

7 Railway construction can transform the economy of remote regions. The Lanzhou–Xinjiang railway was meant to link with Russian railways in the 1960s; though incomplete, its influences on north-western Xinjiang have been remarkable.

8 The line being built from Lanzhou to Lhasa has already speeded up mineral developments in Qinghai.

9 Motor transport comes into its own in areas just beyond the reach of the railways, in the agricultural zones about the big cities, and within the cities themselves.

10 The importance of simple forms of transport to the rural population is still very great. Bicycles, horses-and-carts, handcarts, and trailers, with good wheels, wheelbarrows, and small craft on the waterways are all in constant use, and together move huge quantities of freight.

7 Modern China: the Cities

Urban Expansion and Government Control

Fig. 119 shows the location of China's really large cities, and points to those with more than a million people. During the first ten years of the People's Republic the population of the towns and cities grew three times as fast as China's population as a whole: for the cities had better medical and health facilities than the rural areas, and a lower death rate. Also, the birth rate was higher, for young men and women were attracted to the cities, away from the uncertainties and disasters of the countryside, which added directly to the urban population and introduced more women of child-bearing age.

Large cities which were centres of government, with lots of employees, with better educational opportunities, and serving a well-populated area, grew even more quickly than the smaller ones; so that provincial capitals became several times the size of the next largest city.

The extension of roads and railways often made such cities more suitable places to site industries; so when the government decided to choose key centres for industrial expansion in each region, these were the ones they turned to. They were good focal points for transportation, and so they received many new factories. Thus they grew even larger, by a kind of 'snowball effect'.

The government was faced with problems which have affected cities all over the world ... over-crowding, with pressures on housing, water supply, and sewerage systems and on the streets which once served a much smaller urban area. The huge increase in population in the 1950s and 60s meant that an extra five million jobs were needed each year. Young people found it difficult to obtain useful work in the city.

The government, therefore, tried to slow down the growth of the cities. The first step was to limit the numbers arriving; the next to direct people away from the inner city. Once young people completed their secondary education, they were directed to particular jobs; and so many of them were sent to work outside the urban areas, most to communes close to the suburbs, but some to jobs much further afield. During the period of the Cultural Revolution very large numbers were sent to work in the countryside,

many in 'pioneer areas'. Obviously this was unpopular, and many returned illicitly.

The urban populations still increase, and so, ing therefore, do the problems of unemployment. These are partly counteracted by the proliferation of small private enterprises, and by the more effective results of the 'one-child-only' campaign in urban areas, where preferential treatment in housing and schooling can be given to those who comply.

There is greater mobility of labour, with more people switching from one form of employment to another. But, correspondingly, control over the nature of the small businesses and the life-style of young people in the cities has become more difficult.

Life in the Cities

Where People Live and Work

Most cities now have industrial suburbs spreading out from the old central streets and markets. Although the sites of China's cities differ considerably, there is a general urban pattern. At the centre are the parts of the old city which were once within its walls. Today, the walls have usually gone, and in the centre there are now large, new public buildings, offices, widened roads, squares and parks. About these central business areas many of the old narrow streets remain, where families live in small individual houses which have been renovated, or perhaps share parts of a larger house, built round a courtyard. In the suburbs, there are new residential areas close to modern factories. Here families live in flats; and groups of these buildings, with schools, shopping stores, games areas and public gardens form a neighbourhood unit. The main urban area is divided into districts and sub-districts within which groups of streets are also organised as neighbourhood units. Neighbourhood committees control groups who organise health services, social work, nursery classes, use of sports centres, and so on. They also arrange political classes, and keep a watch over local discipline. Many of the social services are, in fact, staffed by retired workers who are still able to do something useful; for this they

146 This scene in Xian, with frequent public transport (here trolley buses), numerous cyclists, and pavement shelters with posters and papers is typical of most inner cities.

147 The main square at the heart of Xian, with the reviewing stands and adjoining administrative buildings, are also typical of a large city centre. The light traffic does not bother the women chatting, nor those with the handcart.

148 Side streets with their family houses about the administrative-commercial centre of Xian.

149 Part of a free library and recreation centre set up by a neighbourhood committee in a district in inner Chengdu city, for use by young people in the evenings. The TV set, books and various games are provided by sub-district funds.

150 Some of the young people in the part of Chengdu shown in Fig. 149: the girls are interested in new materials.

151 Young children whose parents are working during the day are taken to play in a park in Luoyang.

receive a small extra payment. They also help to arrange activities for children in the school holidays when parents are working. Retirement is usually at sixty.

The large cities have a Bureau which tries to see that families are suitably housed, as far as possible near their work. In fact, life may not be as orderly as it seems. With high youth unemployment, many unattached individuals, and gangs of young people to deal with, urban authorities are often pressed to cope with situations beyond the control of neighbourhood committees.

Committees are also set up in the factories. Some deal with management matters – wage rates, hours of work, production targets etc.; though Party officials are involved in the discussions, to see that state policies are carried through as far as possible. Other factory committees are like the neighbourhood ones; for some large factories provide housing, gas and electricity, water, health services and canteens, and look to the committees to see that the families are cared for, get sick pay, have holidays arranged, and so on.

The provision of nursery schools makes it easier for mothers to go to work. The state subsidises these kindergartens – the helpers being paid by work units – and the parents contribute only a small sum for each child. The children and their parents have certain meals at school or work; but, generally, the family has its evening meal at home, together.

In the early morning the streets and parks are full of people taking exercise, jogging, or doing the slow, stretching movements of Tai Ji Quan (p. 174). Some mothers do their shopping early,

and school children often deliver the smaller ones to nursery class. A parent or relative usually collects them later in the day. The local shops become busy again in the evening, when members of the family are free. Many families now have a TV set; others may watch colour TV at the social centre, or take part in group activities, such as music, drama, or sport. Sunday is a day for shopping, housework and resting, or perhaps visiting a park, taking an outing, or eating out as a family.

Relations with the Surrounding Countryside

The spread of the city over the surrounding rural land is a problem. Agricultural land is needed to supply the city with fresh produce. In many cases the suburbs have taken in small villages, which still have quite a lot of farmland about them. Sites for new factories and workers' homes are often chosen, if possible, on waste ground and hilly areas, leaving flat land for intensive farming within the city boundaries. Thus, on a journey out through a city's suburbs, one usually sees people working on small plots, and in larger fields tending rows of vegetables, and other open spaces covered by long greenhouses.

Rural communities adjoining outer suburbs are often administered as part of the city itself. The municipal areas of large cities may cover a number of counties and sometimes include reservoirs from which water is piped to the city

152 Blocks of flats in a new outer industrial district in Nanning, with people working on plots of land nearby.

(p. 131). The nearby rural lands supply the people in the city with fresh food, and often provide materials for construction from quarries or river beds. Groups of people contract to supply urban markets with chicken, eggs, meat, vegetables or fruit. Apart from these, private enterprise stalls like the streets in certain districts, selling rural produce and a range of other consumer goods.

Where the large municipal areas stretch far beyond the city suburbs, they usually include separate industrial towns, deliberately sited to attract their working population from the city itself. The countryside about the city is usually served by good roads, though only the main highways between towns may be well surfaced.

Transport and Outdoor Life

Public transport within the city includes regular buses, trams or trolley buses. Most people cycle through the streets, parking their machines in neat rows near stores, offices or cinemas. There are trucks and small commercial vans run by businesses, markets, or collectives supplying the city, and also various forms of animal transport. Official cars and taxis add to the traffic, and trucks and buses bring groups of people into the city from the rural areas. The railway station is thronged with travellers, and loud with announcements and music. Families gather

outside, about their bundles and parcels, waiting for the train to take them back to their part of rural China. Children play, and vendors sell buns and fruit, rice gruel and sweets.

The streets are usually lively places. Bright posters point to road safety and health hints, and, now, advertise commercial products. Groups gather about wall posters and long glassed-in panels displaying state newspapers and local information. On the wider pavements the refreshment stalls, with vacuum flasks and mugs for tea-making, sell cakes and sweetmeats. Eating places range from small cafés to busy restaurants which provide hot food; these may have a variety of meals available on different floors. There are many small shops and street markets as well as the big stores.

Well laid-out parks and gardens are a feature of the cities. Here families stroll and take recreation, and groups of retired men sit together playing checkers and other table games, surrounded by onlookers. The large formal squares in the city centre are used for party meetings, young people's rallies, and formal celebrations; and at times become the focal points for groups of earnest debaters, or for protest meetings.

153 Even the old parts of Xian now have small, neat retail stores, like the dress shop on the right.

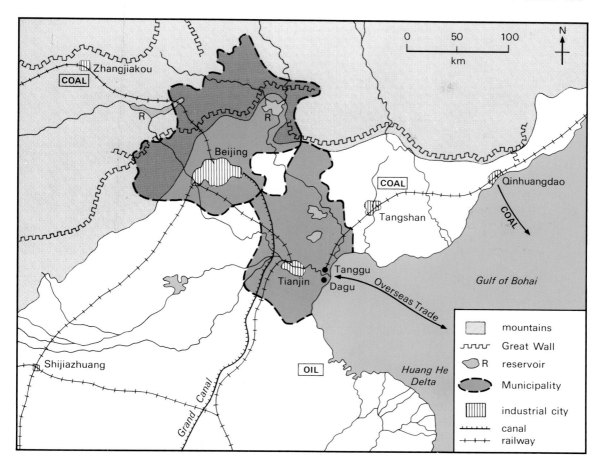

154 *The municipalities of Beijing and Tianjin, with its outports, extend over large areas of surrounding countryside and include many separate towns.*

By looking at a number of larger cities, we can see how well they show this general pattern of urban development. Of course, the location of the city, and its chief functions, will give it certain, special characteristics, but it is usually easy to recognise many of the common features described above.

Beijing (Peking)

The city itself spreads over the north-western part of the lowlands; across which flow the many tributaries of the river Hai, carrying the waters from the western mountains into the Bohai Gulf. At latitude 40°N, the summers are hot and humid; but, as we have seen, its winters are cold and at times the air is very dusty. The actual city and its suburbs are only part of the wide Beijing municipality, which covers 16 800 km² and includes the edge of the mountain country to the north-west of the plain.

The oldest parts of the city we see today were built during the Ming dynasty, from the 14th century onwards; though Beijing had been a capital city under the Mongols. It has been reconstructed and expanded over the last five hundred years. Most of the old outer walls have recently been removed, but the remains of the imperial city stand impressively along a north–south axis of some 8 km, at the centre of modern

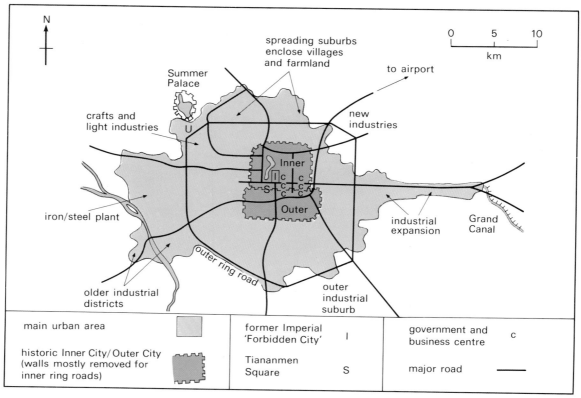

155 The main urban area of Beijing — from the historic core and administrative-business centre, through the old residential inner suburbs, to the outer industrial suburbs and new factory districts. U indicates the urban expansion seen in Fig. 159.

Beijing. The northern part of this is the old Inner City, within which, surrounded by a moat, stands the Forbidden City, the emperor's palace at its heart. South of this are the remains of the Outer City, with two temples used by the emperors for specific ceremonies. The splendours of all these buildings and gardens, and parks and museums created since, are now open to the general public.

The great Tiananmen square opens out before one of the gates to the Inner City; on its other sides stand the Great Hall of the People, the Chairman Mao Memorial Hall, and the fine History Museum. It has been the scene of many rallies and, sadly, recent tragic events. To the east and west runs a wide avenue with imposing, if heavy, rectangular government buildings.

Beijing shows very clearly the historic city centre, now opened out by broad avenues, with modern cultural and administrative buildings. There has also been much reconstruction involving the removal of old houses and the former city walls, to provide wide roads and commercial areas with new shopping centres. But most of the city's fifty parks have been retained, and there is still a maze of old lanes (*hutongs*) near the centre. Many of the shop assistants, government workers, doctors, teachers and others employed within the city live there. Some of the lanes are wide enough to be tree-lined, and behind the trees stand one-storey houses, built around a courtyard; other lanes are very narrow and house types vary in different districts. A residents' committee is usually formed to look after the interests of the families in such a lane.

The outer parts of Beijing are very different, with industrial estates and new factories. To the south-west are the older heavy industries; and newer ones have been built to the east and south, where for much of the year the winds carry away industrial fumes. Much of the lighter manufacturing, with processing plants and handicraft industries, is in the north and north-

156 *Central Beijing, with tall offices and flats, and cyclists streaming along East Chang-an Avenue. Traffic is controlled by lights and by a policeman under the white shade.*

157 *As elsewhere, suburban shopping in Beijing involves purchases from stores and from open markets and pavement displays of fresh produce brought into the city.*

158 *A canal in north-west Beijing which is now used as a reservoir, and for duck farming and fish-breeding for urban consumption.*

159 Factories and high-rise flats spreading over Beijing's outer suburbs to the very edge of the Summer Palace.

west. Here, too, in a pleasant district, are various educational and research institutes, and high-rise flats extend towards the former Summer Palace, a place of recreation whose scenic complex overlooks a large lake (Fig. 159).

Beijing demonstrates the 'linking the city with the countryside' policy. Between the industrial districts are fields of vegetables, orchards, greenhouses, and fish ponds, supplying fresh produce, and receiving city waste as fertiliser. Many of these outer suburbs resemble the villages they once were, with wide stretches of open farmland among them.

Nearly half of Beijing's ten million people live outside the urban nucleus. New satellite towns have been developed within the counties which make up the municipal area. Land use in the counties is as carefully planned as in the city. Large reservoirs in the hills feed irrigation canals which run across the plains. Trees and shelter belts partly protect the fields and buildings against the dry, dust-laden winds of winter. Industrial and agricultural production are intermingled. This is clearly seen on the route north-eastward to Beijing's airport, where greenhouses and orchards alternate with factories, and canals cut across rural land. The satellite towns have their own industries: Fangshan, for example, in very fertile country 60 km south-west of the city, has oil and chemical industries.

Tianjin (Tientsin)

Some eight million people live in the municipality of Tianjin which extends over 13 000 km². The city centre is 120 km south-east of Beijing, near the confluence of five tributaries to the Hai river, which is linked to the northern section of the Grand Canal. As the river silted up, this 19th-century treaty port became ineffective, so that a new port, Dagu (Taiku), was built near its mouth. Today, another outport, Tanggu, on the north bank of the river, handles the growing quantity of container cargo.

The lay-out of Tianjin city is determined by its 16 km frontage along the river. Backing this are the older parts of the city, with the original cotton textile and carpet-making industries close to the waterway, kept open for small craft by dredging. Its suburbs spread far from the old centre, with factories making heavy machinery and vehicles, and a wide range of lighter products, such as electronic instruments and cameras. The city was replanned after the disastrous earthquake of 1976, which wrecked many districts, and destroyed the city of Tangshan, further north. Beyond, a rich grain-growing countryside, produces vegetables, fruits and dairy produce for the urban area.

Shanghai

The old city centre is some 28 km up the river
Huangpu (Whangpoo) from where it flows into
the Chang jiang. Here the Wusong river (Suzhou
Creek) joins the Huangpu and provides a
waterway which runs westward through the city
and across open countryside to link it with the
Grand Canal. Shanghai's docks were built down-
river from the city centre along the banks of the
Huangpu. During the 19th century an
International Settlement was established, just
south of the Wusong river, and each foreign
power claimed a section of the city, and
established commercial buildings along the Bund,
overlooking the Huangpu. European interests
made this treaty port China's chief commerial and
banking centre, a gateway to the huge internal
market. Industries, cotton mills in particular, were
established about the port area, leading to a dense
population, where people lived in a jumble of
small dwellings, in unplanned slum conditions,
inadequately supplied with drinking water and
other facilities: all of which contrasted sharply
with the International Settlement at the river
confluence, with its imposing buildings and broad
streets.

Today, Shanghai still owes a great deal to the
routeway of the Chang jiang and the railways
which give it an enormous hinterland; and it is
now served by two civil airports. Trading and
banking are still important, but it is now an
industrial city, with many thousands of factories,
and research establishments and technical
institutes. Like Beijing and Tianjin, it is directly
administered by the central government, and its
municipality includes rural land to the west, in all
over 6000 km². The city itself is administered
through twelve districts, divided into scores of
neighbourhood units, and well over half of
the twelve million people live in the main urban
area. The docks and many industries have spread
down the Huangpu river. There is an integrated
iron and steel works near its mouth, and oil
refineries and petro-chemical industries have been
built to the east, along the Chang jiang. The heavy
industries, shipyards and thermal power stations
all benefit from their coastal location.

In recent years the government has sought to
redistribute the population, reconstruct the inner

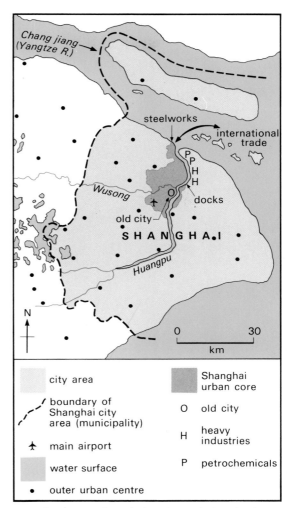

160 *The municipality of Shanghai includes islands in
the Chang jiang estuary and also rural counties and
separate towns west and east of the Huangpu. Heavy
industries and petrochemical plants lie along the lower
Huangpu (Fig. 161).*

city, and move many of the factories and
employees to the suburbs, where new industries
have been set up. The number of people moving
into the city from rural areas has been controlled.
The old town is still a maze of narrow streets, but
the housing has been renovated. New schools,
food markets, and recreation spaces have been
provided. Family planning has dramatically
lowered the inner city birth-rate. Yet, even now,
Shanghai is a bustling, crowded city, and its
central business districts have a livelier air than
most Chinese city centres.

161 *Looking down the Huangpu, across factories, commercial buildings, and ships docked along the west bank to the Chang jiang.*

About the inner city core are industrial estates, with four- or five-storey living blocks of five-room flats, sited about landscaped spaces. Each neighbourhood has markets and stores, medical centres and schools. Buses, and the innumerable bicycles, take people to the city centre, where larger stores offer a wider range of goods. Trucks and pedal carts bring in fresh produce for the city from the open countryside about the main urban area, and successive crops of vegetables are grown on small plots of intensively farmed land in the outer suburbs.

Ten industrial satellite towns have been created within some 20–70 km from the centre of Shanghai. They have absorbed about a million people, thus easing the urban congestion: they also provide employment in specialised industries. Sino-foreign joint venture firms are involved in a number of high-tech industries in and about the city.

Shanghai is a busy bustling city, with a reputation for setting new fashions and being able to offer a wider range of consumer goods than most Chinese cities. There has been a proliferation of small enterprises, with individuals or small groups setting up workshops and small retail businesses. But even so it is not easy for those who complete schooling to find immediate employment. China's recent industrial progress has been great, but there are still limited opportunities for many intelligent young people, even in a big city like this.

Guangzhou (Canton)

The city has always looked to the river; and in the days of European trading rights, finance and

162 *Lighters on the Wusong river (Suzhou creek), which is still an important waterway, flowing eastward through central Shanghai.*

commerce were organised from a river island, where the British and French legations, banks and residences were set apart from Chinese Guangzhou, which had developed on the Pearl river (Zhu jiang) in the northern part of the Xi river estuary. When silting made the old port too shallow, new docks were developed at Huangpu (Whampoa), 18 km down-river; though, even today, silting is a problem. Commerce was the life of the city, and tens of thousands of families lived on boats of the waterways.

The city now spreads far from the massive buildings of its central business district with its stores, offices and restaurants. There are hundreds of factories amid the residential areas which make up the suburbs; but there is a spacious feeling, for

Guangzhou has great open parks; and steep, wooded hills with recreation areas, rise above the outskirts. The hills give broad views of a countryside which is closely farmed, for numerous small enterprises now provide much of the city's daily requirements of food and agricultural raw materials (p. 77). In fact, the city itself exports large quantities of foodstuffs and textiles.

We have already seen something of its early history, its role in the Opium Wars, and its

163 *Guangzhou at the head of the estuary is linked by rail to the Special Economic Zone about Shenzhen and to Hong Kong.*

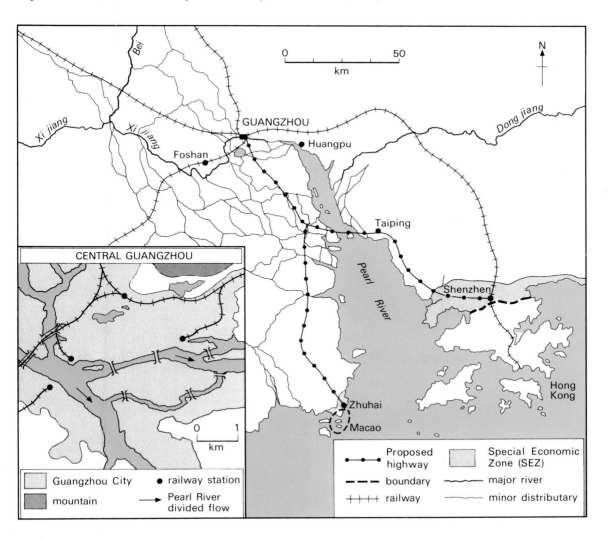

relations with Hong Kong. Today, Hong Kong relies on Guangzhou and its neighbouring countryside for many essentials – water, fresh food and electricity (p. 157). Hong Kong greatly influences Guangzhou, both by its lifestyle and by acting as an inlet for foreign activities. Many overseas Chinese, especially from Hong Kong, visit relatives in and around Guangzhou; large numbers of foreign tourists begin their journeys there, and businessmen visit the city and take part in its frequent conferences. The advantages of joint foreign/Chinese enterprises operating in the Special Economic Zone are considered on p. 112. Guangzhou has a busy airport, and the 180 km rail-link with Hong Kong makes it a good place for China's business fairs, trade conventions, and tourist organisations. Motor highways have been constructed as a joint venture with Hong Kong businesses to link the city with the Special Economic Zones of Shenzhen and Zhuhai.

164 Vehicles bringing produce into Guangzhou from beyond the Pearl river bridge. Plastic raincoats and umbrellas keep off the summer rain.

165 February in Guangzhou, when parks have flower displays and entertainments to celebrate the New Year.

These examples of urban developments have so far related to large eastern cities, three of them developed from former treaty ports. But when we look at cities far inland, with a very different history, and a population made up in many cases of people of different racial groups and contrasting backgrounds, we can still see familiar patterns of lay-out and development. Certainly this is is the case with Kunming.

Kunming

We have already seen that Kunming is the capital of Yunnan province, and an important route centre and manufacturing city, on the edge of the high fertile basin which contains Lake Dian Chi. It was founded as a walled city, early in the 19th century; since then a number of quite unrelated events have contributed to its growth. In 1900 the French built a railway line to it from Indo-China, as part of their drive to obtain copper. During the Japanese war, refugees from the east poured into the city. Then, as industries developed, people moved into Kunming from the Yunnan countryside. It thus acquired a mixture of cultures, for Yunnan has 22 minority groups. Recently the city has received many Vietnamese refugees. But there was no railway link eastward to Guiyang until the late 1960s, so that the whole area retained its isolated regional character.

Today, the city, with its nearby rural areas and satellite towns, has over a million people. Here, again, we see the close combination of settlement, industry and agriculture. The beauty of its natural surroundings, lake and mountains, and careful urban planning, give the large city a feeling of belonging to the countryside. Wide tree-lined roads and landscaped parks have made the older districts more spacious, and in the newer industrial and commercial districts near Lake Dian Chi, there are small lakes with pleasure boats in the parks, and strips of closely farmed land. In the northern suburbs which spread into the valleys of the surrounding hills, are colleges and agricultural institutes, but also occasional factories and blocks of flats; and the suburbs now include older villages, still surrounded by small, intensively cultivated fields. Beyond, the hills contain old temple sites, set in woodland and used as parks. Local people travel long distances to visit scenic places in the high country beyond this lake basin, where a further series of fault basins and spectacular pinnacle-karst country are attracting international tourism.

166 Briquettes of refuse from suburban districts are used as fertiliser on vegetable plots within the city. They are placed in cut-out rectangles and broken down with flails to provide a rich soil.

Points to Consider

1 Towns tend to act as magnets for people in less-developed rural areas. In China rural-urban movements are controlled.

2 Route focuses, such as ports and regional centres, tend to grow as offices and factories are sited there to take advantage of their favourable location. 'Snowball' effects can lead to excessive growth.

3 China, unlike many developing countries, has been able to deal with over-crowding by directing townsfolk to work and settle elsewhere.

4 Small commercial, catering, and service enterprises, banned during the Cultural Revolution, are being encouraged, to create jobs and raise living standards.

5 Life in the city is often overcrowded, and privacy rare. However, neighbourhood committees and elderly relatives can lighten the load for working parents.

6 Housing shortages, employment problems, inflation, especially rising food prices, and rationing are major urban problems (p. 167)

7 In the crowded city, the parks have a special role for cultural activities, as well as providing space for exercise and recreation.

8 The ancient origin of many northern cities is shown by the patterns of old walls, streets and by the buildings. But much of historic interest has been destroyed by modern development.

167 Relaxing with a football beside one of the great gates of the Inner City Wall, now demolished to create a broad road through central Beijing.

8 China and the World Today

Trade and Relations with Other Countries

Over the years the People's Republic has had to buy manufactured goods, machinery, equipment, and certain industrial raw materials, and sell commodities based on agricultural produce, raw and processed – foodstuffs, fibres, textiles, and clothing – and a proportion of minerals. From time to time events have affected the nature of the commodities exported and the pattern of trade. This sequence of changes puts in perspective the present trading situation; for recently the imports have included advanced forms of machinery and equipment, high technology, and foreign services; while petroleum and manufactured goods have become increasingly important earners of foreign currency; and so, to a lesser extent, has the growing tourist industry.

After the break with the USSR in 1960, China had to try to make progress almost on its own, with little help from the other industrialised nations. Political barriers prevented trade with the USA, and there was only limited trade with most European countries and with Japan.

From 1959 to the mid-1960s, concurrent agricultural and climatic disasters (p. 46) caused China to import large quantities of grain from Canada and Australia. With fewer agricultural commodities to sell, China had to cut back on industrial imports (Fig. 168). Table 1 shows the extent of the trade with the grain-exporting countries. Trade with Hong Kong increased; but while imports from the USSR declined, they were not being replaced by those from other industrialised nations.

Towards the end of the 1960s, China began to import more industrial machinery and equipment; mostly those which could improve agricultural output, such as plant to produce chemical fertilisers.

By the late 1970s, the situation had started to change. There was a freer exchange of ideas with the 'West', and expanding trade with Japan. China began to provide opportunities for foreign investors and technicians to help with the development of its industries.

More recently, in order to stimulate its own manufacturing capabilities, China has increased its imports of machinery and high-technological equipment. Joint ventures with foreign firms are helping production, and also providing managerial experience and a knowledge of industrial techniques. Sino-Japanese firms, for instance, began by using imported parts for assembling such things as motor-cycles, electronic equipment, and TV sets; but now, in some instances, Chinese factories are manufacturing the appropriate parts and turning out the complete product.

Trade with Japan has greatly increased, helped by large exports of oil and other minerals. With

168 Categories of imports which show the reaction and readjustment following the break with the USSR.

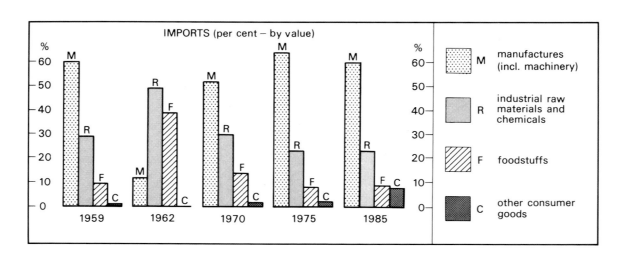

the USA's final recognition of the People's Republic, there was an immediate surge of trade between the two countries; the USA being a grain exporter and able to supply advanced industrial equipment, and also an oil importer.

China's exports have risen considerably, and changed in type. Compared with 1977, when primary products made up about half the exports, by 1985 manufactures accounted for 43 per cent, with textiles and light industrial products to the fore. Besides the exports to Japan and the USA, those to the developing countries have greatly increased, many as re-exports through Hong Kong, which receives the greatest quantity by value.

Japan supplies many of China's imports, followed by the USA. Compared with the volume of exports, the imports from Hong Kong are relatively small, though still three times the value of imports from the grain-exporting countries, Australia and Canada. The importance of foreign trade and investments is obvious, but jeopardised by internal political events, such as those of 1989.

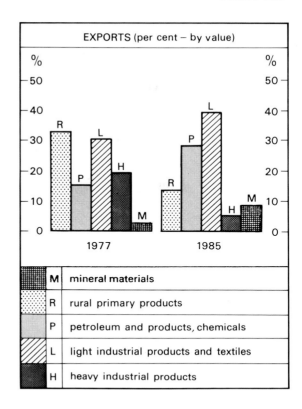

EXPORTS (per cent – by value)

M	mineral materials
R	rural primary products
P	petroleum and products, chemicals
L	light industrial products and textiles
H	heavy industrial products

169 *China's exports are still mainly of primary products (now including petroleum), but with an increasing proportion of textiles and light manufactures.*

Table I
Trade by Countries and Economic Groups (per cent)

	1960	1963		1975	1980	1985
USSR	58	27	Japan	24	24	27
Hong Kong	8	20	Hong Kong	7	14	20
EEC*	10	9	EEC	15	13	11
Japan	1	6	USA	6	13	12
Australia	1	10	Australia	3	3	2
Canada	1	5	Canada	4	4	3
Malaysia/Singapore	1	4	Malaysia/Singapore	4	2	3
USA	—	—	Middle East Oil producers	3	3	2
rest of world	20	19	Third World Countries	11	11	12
			USSR	2	1	
			Other Communist countries	16	8	
(*the present EEC countries)			others	5	4	

170 A silk factory in Sichuan, with girls attaching threads from cocoons in the basins to the spindles above.

Trade with the Developing Countries

China has found it difficult to produce goods which industralised nations might want in return for those they supply. Also, these nations protect their home markets by limiting the quantity of certain goods imported from China. In general, China buys far more from these countries than it sells to them. But, as indicated, this is made up, to some extent, by sales to Hong Kong and the developing countries. China has a large surplus trade balance with these countries, as it does with Hong Kong (Table II). But as it supplies chiefly grain, processed foods, and light manufactured goods the latter must compete with those of Hong Kong, Taiwan, South Korea and some of the developing countries themselves.

Industrialisation and Living Standards

Even before China's recent changes in policy and freer contacts with the 'West', the results of the first struggling programme of industrialisation must be seen as successful by Third World standards. Compared with the 'industrial revolutions' in western countries, there was a very limited increase in capital equipment (industrial machinery and tools) per worker during the first twenty years of the new Republic, yet there was a remarkable rise in productivity. Industrialisation went ahead without a fall in the living standards of industrial workers. This was mainly due to the part played by small industries, with opportunities for workers to influence local decisions. The policy of restricting the growth of urban populations also helped. In fact, both rural and

Table II
Percentage Share of Imports/Exports

	1960	1963	1973–75	1977	1980
Imports: Hong Kong	2	1	3	1	3
Japan	1	7	45	29	26*
Exports: Hong Kong	14	21	26	23	25
Japan	1	6	42	19	22

(*in 1980 the USA supplied 20 per cent)

urban incomes steadily increased, which was certainly not the case in the early days of industrialisation in other nations. But this was only successful industrial and rural development by comparison with other developing countries. China's rural population, especially, has a low income compared with that in the 'Western' nations. Also, some of China's inland regions experienced severe hardships during this period.

Modernisation and Greater Incentives

We must now review the progress since China embarked on the policy of 'four modernisations' – modernising agriculture, industry, science and technology, and defence. In recent years the volume of goods supplied by Japan, the USA and EEC countries has greatly increased; and China now seeks credit, and obtains highly technical industrial and defence equipment. We have seen the internal economic advances since the government ceased to aim at absolute equality throughout China; a policy difficult to achieve even regionally, where one location has natural advantages over another – greater fertility, or particular mineral reserves. In cases where funds from the richer areas went direct to the poorer, and incomes were equalised, producers in the richer regions had little incentive to increase their production. The same applied to under-achievement in industry. Absolute equality in rewards gave little incentive for individual progress, for not everyone has the idealism to feel duty-bound to work to their limits for the benefit of all (especially for those who are obviously doing a great deal less!). The policies outlined on p. 102 now give extra incentives and better rewards for efficiency, and are increasing production. The new technological industries need men and women who are highly educated and trained to take responsibility.

As China's modernisation goes ahead, economic developments are concentrated on selected zones and resources, for the benefit of the national economy. But opportunities for individual incentives are being put into practice. Firstly in the responsibility system as organised through townships in the rural areas (p. 53).

171 Encouraging initiative: the girl is one of a small group which got together to make and mend garments in street markets and small covered workrooms.

Secondly through greater managerial responsibilities in manufacturing industries. And thirdly in the encouragement of small workshops and retail sales units run by groups of young people – 'youth cooperatives' – with investments at small interest rates and help from neighbourhood communities. They are not strictly cooperatives; for members do not have shares, but accept wages and bonuses based on production, from the state. Other enterprises have tax-free inducements to re-invest and profit-sharing subject only to personal taxation.

National policies change, and in China are apt to change abruptly. So there is still a cautious approach towards long-term industrial agreements on the part of foreign businesses. The attractions of China's vast market and need to import

172 Demands for consumer goods is increasing rapidly: the people in this provincial town, Guanxian, are more than adequately dressed, the children's clothes of synthetic materials show variety, and the library is well patronised.

modern technological equipment brought about new relationships between China and the industrialised nations, and an increasing number of joint ventures. But harsh political suppressions appear to justify caution.

The Effects of Population Increase on Trade and Living Standards

China now obtains much foreign currency by exporting more minerals, as well as agricultural products, to the industrialised countries — oil and iron ore to Japan, tin and other non-ferrous metals to Britain, for example — so that anything which will increase or decrease such exports affects the country's modernisation programme. As China's population grows, and the standards of living of the people increase, and with the

success of the 'four modernisations' policy, the country's own requirements of raw materials are increasing. This may bring a fall in raw material exports. On the other hand, despite home demands, it is likely that China's exports of manufactured goods will increase, especially to the developing countries. But, again, China's grain imports remain high; and even though better rewards for producers may stimulate production, as the population grows so does the demand for food.

Despite such uncertainties concerning the economic future, one thing China can attempt to control, with some optimism for long-term benefits, is the rate of growth of the population. China regards the campaign to limit the size of families as a priority. Fig. 173 emphasises the need for this, but also shows that, however successful the restrictions, there will be an increasing population problem for some time yet. This makes it more difficult to improve living standards for the nation as a whole.

There are ceaseless campaigns for one-child families, with rewards and bonuses for the parents; these are reduced if there is a second child. Family planning advice is forcefully put forward. If the one-child family campaign were

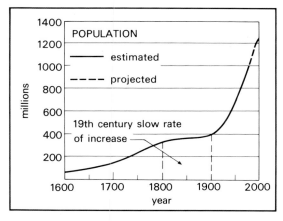

173 *A graph which shows why policies for population control are so important.*

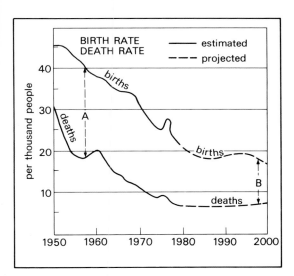

174 *The death-rate fell sharply after the upheavals of the 'forties and as health schemes took effect; and, although the birth-rate fell, by 1957 there was a high rate of population increase (A). Continuing success in birth control should reduce the rate of increase (B).*

successful, then there would be an absolute reduction in population. But the love of children is very strong, and under the responsibility system rural families gain by adding to their labour force. Fig. 174 shows that there has already been a general fall in the birth-rate; and, though this has been countered by health improvements and a falling death-rate, the population is now increasing more slowly: compare A and B in Fig. 174.

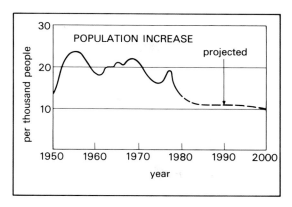

175 *The rate of population increase reflects the conditions described in Fig. 174.*

China's Example and the Developing Countries

China is not a typical developing country. Its size, population, history, political organisation, relations with the industrialised countries, and developments of energy resources have set it aside from other developing countries. Even before the introduction of the Responsibility System, the political and social organisation established during previous generations enabled the government to carry out large-scale projects through the labour of millions of people. For example, their determination to create a 'second Great Wall' of trees to combat erosion, which endangers so much of the farmlands of northern China (Fig. 177). Many millions of trees form shelter belts within agricultural areas.

Like most of the developing countries, but on a larger scale, China had to cope with a vast population of desperately poor peasants: yet now most of them have a standard of living and prospects for the future which seemed out of the question only a short time ago.

China's past successes and the introduction of more liberal policies point to ways in which developing countries can progress: though the methods by which China has been able to forge ahead, may be difficult for other countries to emulate and some of its methods unacceptable. Here, therefore, with comments, are some of the policies and actions which have helped China at various stages of development.

176 A poster in central Chengdu proposes the one-child family as a means of population control.

177 Shelter belts, which would create a 'Great Green Wall' of trees in the north, and areas where afforestation is already part of the campaign to check erosion.

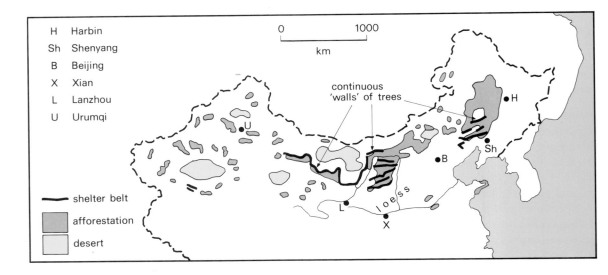

H   Harbin
Sh Shenyang
B   Beijing
X   Xian
L   Lanzhou
U   Urumqi

0   1000
        km

continuous
'walls' of trees

— shelter belt

afforestation

desert

1   Organising some form of collective farming, with a re-distribution of land. (This is difficult in many countries, which have a system of large landowners, tenant farmers and landless labourers.)

2   Keeping a balance between agriculture and industry: distributing equipment and materials which will give agriculture a sound share in the economy. (This is possible in most countries, but depends on a government stable enough to carry out long-term plans.)

3   'Walking on two legs': using *both* large-scale and small-scale industries, and setting favourable prices for the sale of products from small industries. (In developing countries this is often difficult to do because the type of manufacturing depends on foreign investments in industries to produce particular commodities which the investors need, at favourable rates; again it depends on having a government able to carry out long-term plans.)

4   Creating large-scale projects which will improve the country's economy and employ large numbers of people. (This must depend on the present economy of the country, and whether, or not, other nations or world organisations would help to finance such schemes.)

5   Learning skills in agriculture and industry as part of general education. (This should be possible in schools, especially where local technical institutes or demonstrations farms can be set up to encourage intermediate technology.)

6   By decentralising planning and giving more regional control. (This applies particularly to large countries like China, which itself has maintained a balance between very firm central control and adaptations at regional level. Elsewhere, it is so often disrupted by tribal, racial, or religious activities which create problems between one region and another, and between regions and the central government.)

7   Participation by workers in management. (This depends on the educational standard and literacy of the people, as well as on the degree of democracy allowed by the government.)

8   Trying to control the drift to large towns and cities. (This varies with rural and urban conditions in the country concerned; it requires good relations between population and government before people will accept directions to move.)

9   Training paramedics. (This must be applicable to most developing countries — who may train men and women to hold local clinics and be able to diagnose and treat simple ailments; to increase their skills by experience and further training; and to pass patients where necessary to better qualified doctors at better equipped centres.)

10 By introducing a system which allows a required quota of produce for distribution through state channels, yet gives incentives which will allow personal profit to be used for re-investment and to raise living standards. (As in 1, this depends on land tenure, central control, and freedom from the pressures of foreign investments in land-use).

In general, China has achieved these things for a population of a thousand million people. Very strong central government is needed, and a bureaucracy which works – though each of these requirements can lead to serious problems at times. Problems can also be said to have occurred at times in relation to each of these policies (1–9). Take No. 6 for example, not all is sweetness between Han Chinese and minority peoples in Tibet or Xinjiang; for their various minority groups may well appreciate improvements in their standards of living, yet feel that decentralisation ought to give them more say in their own affairs. But, by and large, these policies can be seen to have succeeded in providing widespread material advantages for a fifth of the world's population.

Points to Consider

1 Statistics for China were not always reliable — partly due to the size of the country; partly to the nature of its population; partly to excessive exaggeration of productivity, especially during the Cultural Revolution; partly for propaganda reasons. Recent statistical publications have been more reliable.

2 The overall pattern of China's overseas trade has remained much the same over the years — the export of primary products and light manufactured goods, especially textiles, and the import of manufactures and industrial raw materials.

3 China still buys grain in large quantities.

4 The emphasis on importing plant, machinery and products of high technology is in line with the policy of 'four modernisations'.

5 These policies and changes in political attitudes have greatly increased trade with Japan and the USA.

6 This increase tends to mask the growing trade with the Third World countries, as shown by Table I.

7 Petroleum production is of such importance to China that there are special arrangements for receiving foreign plant and technical help in exploring and exploiting the oil reserves.

8 Joint economic ventures with foreign countries are also likely to affect wholly Chinese enterprises, by improving management methods and suggesting incentive schemes and other business practices.

9 Collective factories and workshops employ nearly a quarter of China's workers. They produce nearly half of the light industrial goods, and four-fifths of the household goods.

10 'Neighbourhood businesses', where people know each other well, and work together locally, have strength. As free markets for industrial products are encouraged, such businesses are proving useful to the economy.

11 Well-educated engineers and technicians are essential for the modernisation programme, and China desperately needs to increase the number of students engaged in higher education. More qualified people are now being given opportunities to study at overseas institutions.

12 China is very different from other developing countries, and fits none of such categories as 'Third World' used to classify the world's nations.

178 A ship in full sail in the channel between Kowloon and Hong Kong island (beyond), on waters where large merchant vessels and fast hydrofoils are more common sights.

9 Chinese Overseas

Hong Kong

In 1842, by the Treaty of Nanking (p. 39), Britain acquired this rocky island of 83 km², off the Pearl river estuary which led to Canton; and in 1861 persuaded China to cede the peninsula of Kowloon, 10 km² of mainland opposite Hong Kong island, together with another small island, so that the British could control the deep, protected harbour.

In 1898, Britain leased another 932 km² of mainland for a period of 99 years (until 1997), and so added what it called the *New Territories* to the colony. Hong Kong thus had protection inland, and had acquired an area with villages and farmland and supplies of fresh water. The New Territories also include various islands, the largest being the mountainous Lan Tau.

The New Territories are crossed by several ranges of steep, broken hills, with peaks over 900 m; but there is a flat alluvial plain to the north-west, and across this runs the boundary with China, part of it following the small Shumchun river.

Granites form much of the surface of the mainland and islands. In places, hardened volcanic outpourings overlie the granite, as on the higher parts of Hong Kong island. The hot, moist conditions cause the granites to weather and, on breaking up, their particles form a thick debris. Summer storms can be torrential; as much as 630 mm of rain has fallen on a single day. The storm waters have caused much erosion on cleared land, and carry loads of loose particles into the reservoirs. Where water storages are threatened, there are attempts to re-afforest the hillsides, for most of the former forest cover has been removed; and land not built over, or used for farming, now only bears coarse grass, scrub or low bushes.

179 The surface geology of Hong Kong island and the New Territories, which has strong influences on urban and rural land-use and water storage.

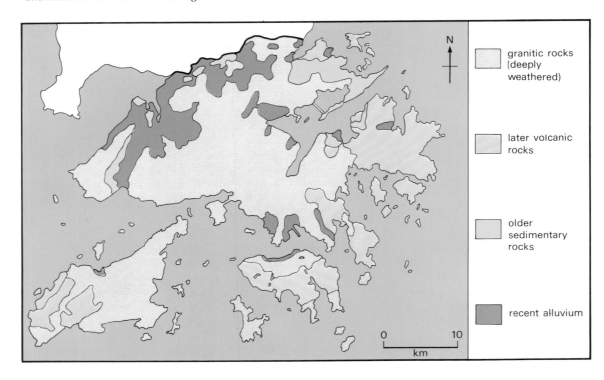

granitic rocks (deeply weathered)

later volcanic rocks

older sedimentary rocks

recent alluvium

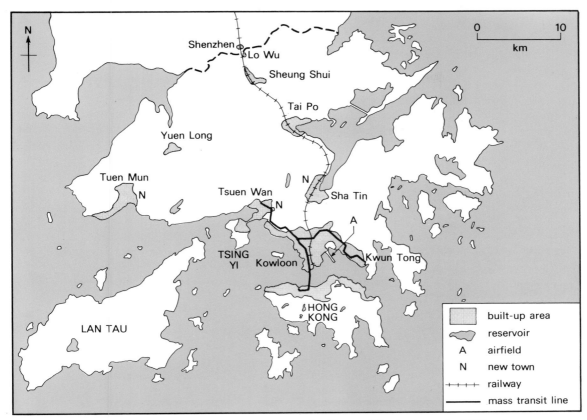

180 Most of the densely populated urban areas are served by the railway to Guangzhou and the new Mass Transit lines, which are being extended.

The Growth of Commerce and Industries

The first centre of settlement was at Victoria, on the north-west of Hong Kong island. This is now a huge high-rise modern city, spreading along much of the north coast. Across the harbour, Kowloon has also grown spectacularly since World War II; and beyond, in the New Territories, expanded settlements and new, planned towns are being created to house millions of people.

For a hundred years, until 1941, Hong Kong was a free port, charging no import duties. It was a great entrepôt, shipping out and receiving raw materials and goods passing between eastern Asia and the rest of the world. The colony became a flourishing commercial centre, well placed in relation to the ports of China, Japan and south-east Asia.

After the disruptions of the war with Japan and

the Korean War in the early 1950s, there was a slump in trade; but, partly as a result of this, there was a drive to set up manufacturing. Trade picked up, but industry had come to stay. Many factories were built, especially in and around Kowloon. Some were very large, many just small workshops; but between them they turned out textiles and garments, and an enormous number of light industrial products of metal, leather, wood, plastic and ceramics. Hong Kong's craft industries flourished, and printing and many forms of replica artwork attracted orders from all over the world.

Today, the commercial centres of Victoria and Kowloon have extremely high land values, and have become a forest of high-rise offices, hotels and stores. Every street has retail shops packed with consumer goods – cameras, watches, electronic apparatus, garments, artwork etc., and overhead is a multitude of colourful advertising signs. These reflect the bustling activity which succeeds in producing highly specialised articles for export, often on contract for firms with a world-wide reputation.

181 *The high-rise buildings of the commercial Central District of Hong Kong island, with Victoria Peak in the background.*

182 *The signs across this Kowloon street emphasise the brashness of the business and entertainment aspects of the colony and the vast sales of cameras, electronic equipment and luxury goods.*

183 The Aberdeen reservoir on Hong Kong island at the end of the dry season. Beyond the blocks of flats is a thermal power station.

Population Problems

Living space has become a problem. The cost of a flat near the centre has become very high. Beyond the central districts are tall tenement blocks of flats, many of them subsidised by the government. In the older parts, there are crowded living quarters above streets crammed with retail stores, workshops, and small offices. The population increase continues to put great pressure on Hong Kong's living space, and on employment, water supply and sanitation facilities.

Political upheavals have brought inflows of refugees from eastern Asian countries, probably more than a million of them since the mid-1960s. Keeping out illegal immigrants has been a great problem. The glitter of Hong Kong attracts many mainland Chinese. Its advantages are talked about by Hong Kong Chinese visiting their relations in Guangdong, and its TV stations can be picked up on the mainland. The apparent attraction of a big city acts as a magnet in most parts of the world, especially where a large rural population has a modest standard of living; and movements to the city usually result in urban overcrowding and

problems of unemployment. On top of this 'pull' towards the city, and the 'push' which has sent so many refugees to Hong Kong, there has been a very high urban birth-rate, though in recent times this has dropped sharply.

The total land area of Hong Kong island and the New Territories is 1052 km^2, and together they contain more than five million people. One closely populated part of Kowloon has a density of some 150 000 per km^2. Despite the rapid building of huge blocks of housing, numerous squatters live in cabins built onto the hillsides about Victoria and in the New Territories. Some 50 000 live on small boats moored in bays and coves and, like the others, await rehousing in government subsidised flats on resettlement estates. As they move out, new arrivals move in. Yet, wherever they live, the people tend to play a full part in urban life, setting up small workshops, sending children to school. In fact, living on boats has long been a way of life for many of Hong Kong's fishing population; now, apart from the inshore fisheries, there is a deep-sea fishing fleet based on Hong Kong.

184 Towering blocks of flats at Sha Tin on mainland New Territories. New Towns are being rapidly developed to cope with the increasing population.

Transport and Urban Expansion

A city such as this needs careful continuous planning, with provisions for rapid modern communications. While ferries still operate continuously between the island and mainland, the multi-storey buildings on either side of the harbour are now linked by road tunnels and by the underground Mass Transit Railway (MTR), which is being extended into the New Territories from Kowloon.

In this way millions of people move from their homes to work-places and shopping centres each day. There are regular bus and coach services, thousands of mini-buses which carry more than a million passengers a day, and numerous taxis. Trams operate on the north shore of Hong Kong island. The runway of the international airport extends from the peninsula, over reclaimed land, far into the harbour.

To overcome the housing shortage, industrial new towns have been created in the New Territories, and existing market towns are being expanded. Each of the towns shown in Fig. 180 aims to house more than a million people, and so keep urban expansion to particular places. Two others are being developed. Much of this development is on land cut from the hillsides or reclaimed from the sea. At Sha Tin, the material removed from the hillsides has been used to fill in

and reclaim nearby inlets. The future development of Lan Tau island, with linking bridges, seems only a matter of time.

The New Towns have huge, cross-shaped 30-storey tower blocks of flats, each able to house 8000 people. The planners try to blend the blocks with the existing houses, temples and fields, using raised walkways for easy access. Many people commute to work elsewhere in the city, though local factories and workshops have been set up. Some relate to the almost continuous development of the harbour itself, the oil terminals, and power stations. Tsuen Wan overlooks one of the world's largest container terminals; and its people now work in shipyards, as well as in textile and chemical industries. Tuen Mun is already developing heavy industries. Fig. 180 also shows those older towns which are being expanded by the addition of new housing and industries. Two of them lie along the railway which runs for 33 km from Kowloon's main station to Lo Wu on the China border, and then on to Guangzhou. Because of the recent increase in the number of people moving between Hong Kong and Guangzhou and the expansion of settlement in the New Territories, it became necessary to replace the single line to the border with double tracks, provide extra trains, re-build the intermediate stations, and electrify the railway. Across the border the Shenzhen Special Economic Zone, with its expanding industrial estates, is linked to Guangzhou by rail and by a new highway.

The Port

The Port itself has changed its cargo-handling facilities in recent years. The Kwai Chung container terminal now handles more than half the cargo. The advantages to ship charterers and the shipping companies is immense, for time spent in port is extremely expensive. Container ships spend, on an average, only 21 hours at berth, compared with 67 hours taken by other commercial ships to complete their loading or unloading.

185 Intensively farmed arable areas in the New Territories. Water is obtained from China by pipeline as well as from the reservoirs and desalination plant.

The sheltered harbour is one of the largest in the world, with moorings for more than seventy ships, which can be refuelled from shore bases and floating oil terminals. Lighters and mechanised junks add to the harbour traffic. There are minor shipyards, and dry docking facilities on the island of Tsing Yi.

Supplies from the Mainland

Wherever possible, there is intensive cultivation in the New Territories. The better land is in the north-west, where as many as eight vegetable crops are taken from the soil each year. Even so, Hong Kong draws on the People's Republic for supplies of fresh food. Altogether, China sends vegetable and animal foodstuffs, textiles and fabrics, and a variety of manufactured consumer goods to Hong Kong, which is its largest single export market; many of the commodities are re-exported (Table IV). Power cables and pipelines bring in electricity and water, imported from the

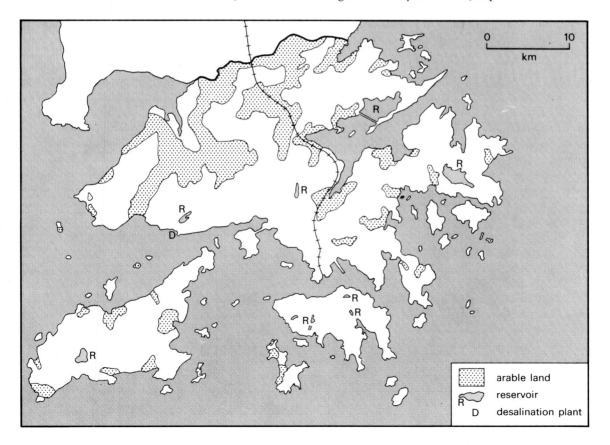

	arable land
R	reservoir
D	desalination plant

186 *Available farmland in the New Territories is intensively cultivated. These coastal flats on mountainous Lan Tau island are carefully irrigated for vegetable crops.*

People's Republic. There are large dammed-up water storages on Lan Tau island and on the mainland New Territories, where a large cove in the north-east has been enclosed to act as a reservoir. There is also a desalination plant which takes salt water from the Pearl river and lifts it to a reservoir inland. But China's Dong jiang is still a main source of supply.

The Chinese government has long had holdings in Hong Kong stores, banks, insurance firms, and other interests, and much investment in Shenzhen has come from Hong Kong businessmen. Funds also reach China in the form of remittances sent by Hong Kong Chinese to their relatives in the People's Republic. They return in increasing numbers to visit relatives in Guangzhou and other parts of southern China, especially at holiday times and festivals. Foreign currency is also sent to the People's Republic by the relatives who live in other countries.

Hong Kong's Functions Today

Hong Kong's unique position, then, in relation to China and to Pacific trade routes, has had much to do with its prosperity and its great recovery after the setbacks of the 1940s. It is a financial centre, with commercial banks and stock markets; it also earns from tourism; and the nature of its trade is summarised in Tables III and IV.

Table IV shows how Hong Kong's earnings depend on the export of manufactured goods, mostly from imported materials, and also on a re-export trade. In 1985 China supplied a quarter of the imports, closely followed by Japan; the USA, Taiwan, and Singapore were the next most important sources. Nearly half the exports went to the USA; China took a quarter of the rest, with West Germany and the UK important customers. But of the re-exports China took almost a half, the USA about a seventh, and most of the rest went to other Asian countries which, besides Japan, included Indonesia, Singapore, Taiwan, Macao, the Philippines, and South Korea – showing Hong Kong's value in re-distributing goods among Pacific countries.

Table III
Imports (per cent) 1985

Electrical, sound equipment; cameras, watches	23
Textiles, fabrics, fibres	16
Basic manufactures	13
Food, live animals	10
Machinery, transport equipment	9
Chemicals	7
Petroleum, products	5
Minerals, metals	3
Misc. manufactures	6
Others	8

Table IV
Exports (Domestic and Re-exports) (per cent) 1985

Domestic

Textiles, clothing	22	
Electrical, sound equipment; cameras, watches	13	
Misc. manufactures	10	
Basic manufactures	5	
Machinery, transport equipment	4	
Others	1	(55)

Re-exports

Textiles, clothing	11	
Electrical, sound equipment; cameras, watches	9	
Machinery, transport equipment	6	
Basic manufactures	5	
Misc. manufactures	5	
Chemicals	3	
Food, live animals	2	
Others	4	(45)

1997 – The Return to the People's Republic

It has been agreed that in 1997 Hong Kong will become a Special Administrative Region within the People's Republic of China, and that most citizens will cease to be British Dependent Citizens and become Chinese nationals. China has agreed to a continuation of Hong Kong's social, economic, legal and other systems for at least 50 years from that time. China will undoubtedly wish to retain Hong Kong's importance in world trade and its value as an international finance centre; though there are now serious anxieties among its residents and business houses.

Macao (Macau)

Macao is a Portuguese colony at the mouth of the Pearl river, some 55 km from Hong Kong. It is made up of a small peninsula only five kilometres long by one kilometre wide, connected to the mainland by a neck of land, and also two islands. The Portuguese established a trading station there in 1516, and declared it Portuguese territory in 1849, (confirmed by treaty in 1887). During the early 19th century all European-Chinese trade had to pass through Guangzhou (Canton), and, later, Hong Kong was ceded to Britain, so that Macao had little chance of becoming a major European trading base. In 1999 the territory will become part of The People's Republic. Today, it has nearly half a million people, but acts mainly as a tourist and gambling resort, with visitors arriving by hydrofoil from Hong Kong. Tourism is also important to Zhuhai, the Special Economic Zone across the border.

Taiwan

The mountainous island of Taiwan lies across the Tropic of Cancer, about 160 km from mainland China. It is some 370 km long, from north to south, with an average width of about 120 km. Its population is some 20 million; more than two million live in the capital city, Taibei (Taipei), in the north, and another million in Gaoxiong (Kaohsiung), its main port, in the south-west.

The forested mountain ranges which run north–south through the eastern half of the island are separated by a narrow rift valley from the steep volcanic range which plunges to the ocean depths along the east coast. In the west, a belt of inland hill country gives way to an alluvial plain, the main area of settlement, up to 45 km wide. Rivers wind across the plain and build deltas along the low west coast, where there are occasional lagoons and mangrove swamps.

The forests which covered both the hill country and the plains have mostly been cleared for cultivation. Unfortunately, tree felling has caused parts of hills and lower mountain slopes to become badly eroded. This was the result of indiscriminate felling to obtain valuable camphor

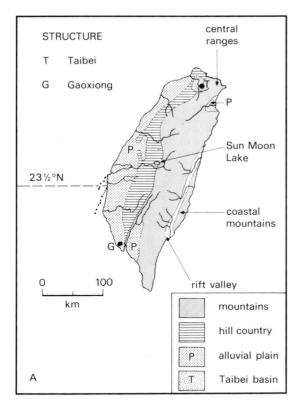

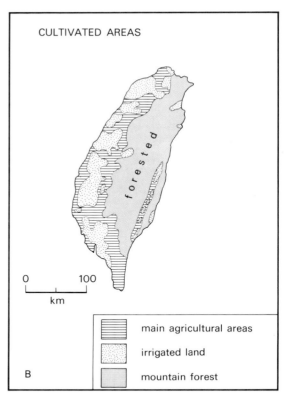

187 Taiwan: mountains restrict most of the agriculture to the western lowlands and the narrower eastern valleys.

trees; but a more careful use is now made of forest resources, and plywood and furniture are important exports.

History of Settlement

Groups of Chinese began to colonise the island during the 15th century AD. In the 16th century, Portuguese sailors gave it the name 'Ilha Formosa' – 'beautiful island', and for a while, the Portuguese and then the Dutch strove to maintain settlements there. But in the mid-17th century, mainland forces, under a Ming general, drove out the Dutch. In the years that followed nearly two million Chinese came to the island, fleeing from Manchu rule. Even so, by 1683 the Manchus had taken control and made it part of Fujian province. During the 19th century, the Europeans and Japanese became interested in it; and, despite the Chinese creating it a province in its own right, Japan took over the island after defeating the Chinese in 1895 (p. 39).

After the removal of the Japanese in 1945, Taiwan was ruled for a time by the Chinese Nationalist government (KMT). In 1949, well over a million Chinese fled from the mainland to settle there under the Kuomintang leader, Chiang Kai-shek, and it became known as the Taiwanese Republic of China. Now it is no longer recognised as such by the United Nations Organisation: but its capitalist society stands on its own feet economically, and its people have experienced a rising standard of living.

Reconciliation with the People's Republic still seems a long way off. When Chiang Kai-shek died in 1975, his son Chiang Ching-kuo became Prime Minister, and the policy of high spending to maintain highly trained and well-equipped armed forces, aiming eventually to return to mainland China, continued. But there are signs that such a policy is less attractive to the young generation of Taiwanese, who appreciate the economic progress being made on the island. Overtures have come from the mainland, and sporting and cultural contacts have been made. The People's Republic aim at a long-term reunification, and, of course, regard Taiwan as part of China.

Rural Development

The people live mainly on the western parts of the island, where most of the agricultural land lies: although economic growth has been in manufacturing industries rather than agriculture. The western plains are usually planted with two rice crops a year, with a winter catch crop. Sweet potatoes and soya beans are also widely grown. The main cash crop, sugar, is exported in quantity, and so, today, are less traditional crops, such as asparagus and mushrooms, which are canned. In the lower hill country, bananas are the chief cash crop, and tea in the northern hills. The small farmers also get a profitable income from citrus fruit, papayas, mangoes and pineapples.

The Japanese did much to develop agriculture. They organised water catchment and irrigation schemes, and improved road and rail communications. They also began to develop the island's great hydro-electric potential, with major projects based on water held in the large Sun Moon Lake, which lies in a faulted depression in the central ranges. These developments have been extended by the present government.

Industrial/Commercial Growth: American Investment

Until 1965, the Taiwan government received much financial help direct from the USA. Now many of its development projects receive support and direct investment from leading American firms and banks, and the island has satisfactory reserves of foreign exchange. As a result of this continued support, the government put forward a series of Plans to achieve progress. They looked first to improving agriculture; next to

188 *Besides these traditional cash crops, a variety of vegetables and fruits are profitably grown in western Taiwan.*

189 *Relief has strong influences on the river pattern, energy developments and the railway system.*

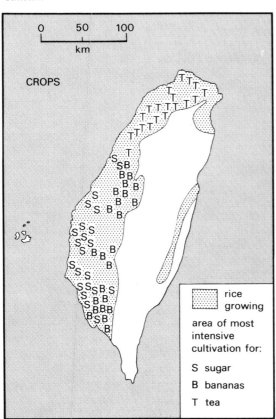

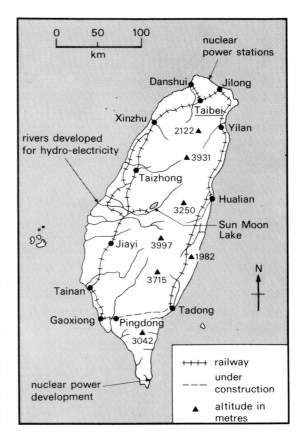

190 Taibei's hotels, shops, and traffic recall Hong Kong rather than Beijing.

developing light industries; and then to using light industries; and then to using modern technology and to expanding heavy industries.

The first series of four-year Plans aimed at agricultural improvements, based on the redistribution of much government and private land to small owner-farmers. In some ways this proved a drawback: for the farms remained small, or became smaller as land was inherited. Cooperative schemes were tried, without complete success: co-operating to make local improvements, such as terracing or water control, proved less effective than in mainland China. Nevertheless, through introducing improved farming techniques, larger irrigation schemes, and applications of chemical fertilisers produced on the island, crop outputs improved considerably. Moreover, as opportunities in industrial employment increased, people left the land, and it was possible to make bigger farms, introduce new techniques and more mechanisation, and encourage people to grow a wider range of crops. Pig-breeding, too, has become a profitable large-scale industry.

The next step was to establish light industries, improve communications and build ports. Labour

was cheap and plentiful, and people worked longer hours than in other countries making similar products. Production came from small workshops with perhaps ten or twenty employees, as well as from large factories set up by overseas investment. Soon Taiwanese products were able to compete on world markets. Private investment in industry was encouraged by loans and tax reliefs, and firms were given help to obtain foreign equipment. Textile industries were established with raw materials and investment from the USA.

Factories in and around Taibei (Taipei) and Gaoxiong (Kaohsiung) at first produced mainly textiles, toys and footwear. But by the end of the 1970s, forty industrial districts had been specially created, mostly in the western parts of the island, and their products ranged from small articles in metals and plastics to machine parts, electrical and electronic apparatus, calculators, TV sets, and diesel engines. Economic planning then concentrated on heavy industrial projects. It proposed nuclear power developments to supplement energy produced by the hydro-electric stations and by natural gas, which supplies thermal stations; a new international airport; new seaport development; and extended railways and motorways. At Gaoxiong there are now refineries, petrochemical and aluminium works, and shipbuilding; and shipyards on Peace Island of

191 *The old Chinatown district in Singapore is picturesque, but fast disappearing under the advance of high-rise flats, offices and hotels.*

Jilong (Chilung), the small northern port, now build oil tankers and bulk carriers.

Such progress has undoubtedly been due to the initial help from the USA, and to overseas investors, again mostly from North America. It has been accompanied by progress in education; so that almost all Taiwanese are now literate, and more and more have the technical training to help them maintain the rise in living standards. But now, as wages have risen, Taiwan does not have the same advantage over competitors as it had when it made fairly simple cheap products: as a result it now turns to producing a wider, specialised, more costly, range of export goods.

The sprawling city of Taibei (Taipei) is a bustling one, with sharp contrasts between its various districts. Its broad central streets, with modern commercial buildings, and side streets with stores and supermarkets are noisy with motor cycles and scooters, and crowded with private cars. Beyond the commercial heart of the city are older districts whose street activites, open-air markets and food stalls, one-room workshops, and craftsmen working in rooms which open onto the broad pavements resemble those of the mainland city suburbs.

Points to Consider

1 Hong Kong's location in relation to ocean trade routes, and to China's great port, Guangzhou, and its own fine harbour facilities have helped to make it a prosperous financial/commercial city.
2 Manufacturing has added to Hong Kong's stability. Like Taiwan, success with light industrial products has led to production of more precise and expensive products, and some heavy industrial development.
3 Hong Kong's dependence on the mainland for water, energy, and fresh food will continue after 1997, when its material prosperity, world-wide financial connections are likely to assure the continuance of its present role.
4 Taiwan's uncertainties derive from lack of international recognition, the attitude of young Taiwanese, and China's low-profile treatment of its 'province'. Industrial developments and overseas investments continue to strengthen its independence.

Chinese Settlements in Other Countries

Apart from the large numbers of Chinese in Hong Kong, Chinese immigrants and their descendants have come to make up a sizeable proportion of the population of many countries in south-east Asia, where their total population is somewhere between 15 and 20 million.

In the Malayan peninsula, for example, Chinese settlers arrived in varying numbers from the 14th century onwards. For some, the reason was to send tin to China, for preparing joss-sticks. But, later, great numbers arrived during the period of British administration, passing through China's southern ports and Hong Kong, to find work in tin mining and dredging. Most came to work as labourers, but many became merchants and shopkeepers. The Chinese dominated the trading towns and villages, which served not only their Chinese communities but also the large numbers of Indian immigrants working on timber estates and rubber plantations. On the whole, they kept themselves apart from the Malayan communities and ran their own schools. They also strongly influenced the development of the large towns and ports, especially the great trading city-port of Singapore, where they had moved into commerce. Today, two-thirds of West Malaysian towns are dominated by the Chinese community. In the various Malaysian territories the Chinese make up roughly half the population, with the largest proportion in West Malaysia and the smallest in the Borneo territories. Singapore is, and has long been, 'Chinese'. Its citizens include Malays and Indians, but the Chinese make up three-quarters of the population of this prospering industrial-commercial city.

For similar reasons, the Chinese built up their numbers in Thailand, Burma, Vietnam, Indonesia, the Philippines and other parts of Malaysia. In fact, each south-east Asian country has immigrant communities of Chinese.

Since independence from colonial rule, there have been problems between the different racial groups in many of these countries, most of which now have strict immigration regulations. The Chinese have faced considerable hostility in Indonesia, for example. Even where they form a minority of the population in these countries, their industry, business sense, and cooperation with each other make them a powerful group of citizens.

The spread of Chinese emigrants has been world-wide, though in smaller numbers than in south-east Asia. There are notable concentrations in many foreign cities: the Chinatown of San Francisco is a well-known example, but there are sizeable communities in towns in the Caribbean islands, in New York and London, in cities in Peru and Sri Lanka, and many other parts of the world.

The People's Republic has taken the view that Overseas Chinese are absent citizens of the homeland (China). Certainly, a large number of them feel closely associated with the homeland of their ancestors: and, more practically, may remit money to relatives in China. Many of those who have returned have been settled in the southern provinces of Fujian and Guangdong. Most of them however, have come as refugees from neighbouring parts of south-east Asia. During the long struggles in Vietnam and Laos in the nineteen sixties and 'seventies, many of their Chinese population returned as refugees to the People's Republic.

China: the Thousand Million – A Summary

People – Not Masses

A figure like 'a thousand million' hides the fact that the nation is made up of individuals and families, and, though they share a Chinese culture developed over thousands of years, and now belong to a communist society, they are far from being a faceless mass: the liveliness in streets and

192 A street library in old Xian with a group totally absorbed in their books – a reminder of the drive towards total literacy in China.

markets, stores and parks is there to be seen.

Nevertheless, the need to conform with broad ideals which have brought great benefits is generally understood by the people, who appreciate that China has achieved these through its own efforts, with the minimum of foreign aid. This contrasts greatly with most Third World countries, which depend heavily on help from the industrially developed countries.

While the people live in a more ordered society than most 'Westerners' do, the human side comes through very strongly. However industrious people may be, there are the usual reactions to frustrations, but also much humour, and enjoyment of leg-pulling, entertainment, and competitive skills. Fig. 192 is also a revealing picture in a country where two generations ago only one in five could read or write.

193 The women show a cheerful approach to spring tasks in the loess lands – their status very different to that in the past.

194 Changing technology is reflected by the wares of this pipe-smoking villager in Xiobanqiao market, who watches over a stock of machine parts instead of the more traditional rural tools and implements.

196 A lesson in basic chemistry in a school attached to a factory is a step towards a technical education. But there are still far too few opportunities for good secondary and tertiary education and training in more advanced technology.

The Party and government have to decide how to allow the youthful population to express itself, achieve further freedoms, and acquire more

195 The vitality of China's predominantly rural population is represented by the rugged health and serviceable clothes of this couple dealing in vegetables and livestock.

material wealth without undermining what has been gained so far. This is one of the reasons for the relatively harsh treatment of those who do not fit into the kind of life planned to maintain progress. There has been much relaxation of restrictions in recent years; but there is also concern lest some sections take unfair advantages of this.

Progress has also been slow in some respects. The annual population increase is still a serious drawback, for ten million persons *extra* each year must slow down the rate of improvement for the others. The frustrations of unemployed young people, and the difficulties of providing educational facilities fast enough, are reasons why many of the controls are not relaxed as quickly as the government may wish. They are dealing with people and their problems on a scale which no other nation faces. Concern for the people is best seen at the family level — through the health services and social benefits, but there is ruthlessness in dealing with deviations from central party and government policy.

197 (overleaf) Table tennis surfaces are set up in most playgrounds and parks throughout the country, and, of course, China has many world-class players.

Liberal policies have brought about economic advantages at village level and at national level, but not without potentially destabilising side effects, which the very scale of the changes and the size of the country make it difficult to control and adjust.

Private merchants can now take produce to wholesale centres other than those organised by the state-county system. Produce can be transported from the producing area to meet local requirements in other parts of the country. The growth of a free market system has generated a network of wholesale markets with private merchants dealing in free-market goods. This has stimulated other economic activities in goods-handling, communications, banking, and financial services. This means extra employment and the incentive to increase individual incomes, but also loopholes for inevitable sharp practices. The government seeks to control the latter without stifling initiative.

There are now incentives for peasants not only to grow what will fetch the highest prices, but to sell at markets which offer the best returns when transport costs are deducted. In urban markets long-distance traders, wholesalers and retailers include private merchants, peasant cooperatives, and state units. In some large cities, like Shenyang and Chongqing, wholesale markets are establishing offices in distant provinces and cities.

The growth in rural and urban incomes, and the increasing population, mean ever greater demands for produce, which can not always be met. Shortages have caused steep price increases in many commodities; so that urban families, faced with inflation, begin to envisage a fall in living standards. Attempts to limit prices paid to farmers for particular types of produce have caused them to switch to more profitable activities, so creating a greater shortage of those commodities. During 1987, stores in many cities re-introduced rationing of pork, eggs and sugar.

The government thus has to consider increasing urban wages, or providing subsidies which will reduce prices in urban markets. Yet they must allow producers to receive better returns on commodities in short supply, particularly as the retail price of such things as diesel fuel, tools, greenhouse-sheeting, fertilisers and pesticides has also soared, affecting the farmers' income.

In other fields the reforms include greater opportunities for borrowing by local enterprises from branches of state banks or credit cooperatives, and loans from foreign sources for firms involved in approved industrial development, especially in the field of high technology. Land for this kind of development in an open economic zone may now be leased on a long-term basis. The attitude to land ownership has also changed in respect of family housing. To redress serious urban housing shortages, a real estate market is being developed, allowing families to buy or lease apartments and houses.

The results of such liberalisation policies during the last decade have meant greater freedom for enterprising individuals and collectives, and an overall rise in living standards for the majority of the population; though with slower progress in the more inaccessible parts of the country. They have, however, set a whole range of new social and economic problems for the country's leaders, who continue to modify policies to meet the changing circumstances, and attempt to control those who will inevitably seek to exploit the greater freedoms. The government's top-heavy bureaucracy, which has hampered the implementation of many of the new policies, is being improved by streamlining the government departments; and particularly by delegating the mangement of enterprises to lower levels, where the practical problems can be more readily appreciated and dealt with. But there remains much dissatisfaction with the influence of party-appointed individuals on major policy decisions, and the inability of citizens and rural communities to express themselves through democratically elected officials. When putting China's problems and progress in global perspective, it is important to remember that over a thousand million individuals are involved, and that the ruling party obviously fears the consequences of loosening controls and conceding local democratic reforms which might conflict with central policies for the country as a whole.

Appendix

199 Climatic data available.

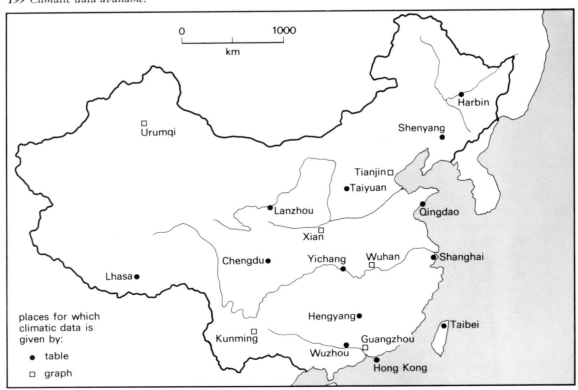

Climatic Data

Mean Monthly Temperatures and Precipitation

Sets of data which, with those shown in Fig. 14, give an idea of the regional climatic variations within China.

	J	F	M	A	M	J	J	A	S	O	N	D	T		Location
Harbin	−18	−11	−4	5	13	19	22	21	15	4	−6	−13	(34/−35)	°C	far north-east
	4	6	10	24	43	94	110	103	46	33	8	5	480	mm	
Shenyang	−12	−8	−1	9	16	22	25	24	17	9	−1	−9	(36/−25)		far north-east
	8	9	18	29	68	83	180	168	63	35	28	15	698		
Taiyuan	−7	−3	1	11	18	22	25	23	18	11	2	−5	(36/−22)		north-east
	3	3	5	10	28	55	115	110	43	13	−	2	387		
Lanzhou	−7	−1	5	11	17	20	23	22	16	10	2	−3	(36/−18)		north-west
	5	6	8	13	20	18	83	128	56	15	2	8	353		
Chengdu	6	8	11	16	24	35	26	25	22	17	18	8	(34/0)		Sichuan
	5	8	14	48	60	113	218	288	158	53	13	5	983		basin
Lhasa	−3	1	4	8	12	17	16	15	14	9	5	0	(28/−15)		Tibetan
	−	13	8	6	24	63	120	88	65	13	3	−	403		valley
Qingdao	−1	0	4	8	16	20	23	26	22	18	8	2	(32/−11)		north-central
	8	11	19	38	40	82	153	145	84	33	20	15	648		(coastal)
Yichang	6	7	11	18	22	26	29	29	25	19	13	8	(41/−3)		central
	23	30	49	98	123	157	205	175	100	73	33	18	1078		(river basin)
Hengyang	4	7	13	16	24	26	30	30	27	19	13	8	(41/−5)		south-central
	68	132	92	191	165	262	84	143	62	82	118	51	1450		(river basin)
Shanghai	4	5	8	14	20	23	28	28	24	18	12	9	(37/−7)		central
	48	58	83	93	94	178	145	140	128	72	50	35	1118		(coastal)
Wuzhou	11	13	16	22	26	28	29	29	27	23	19	15	(36/2)		south
	32	55	95	158	202	190	157	175	83	43	38	37	1265		(river basin)
Hong Kong	16	15	17	21	25	27	29	28	27	25	20	17	(34/6)		south
	33	44	73	135	288	386	375	355	252	113	43	30	2127		(coastal island)
Taibei (Taipei)	16	15	17	21	24	27	29	28	27	23	20	17	(36/5)	°C	south
	85	113	175	168	227	285	227	300	240	120	65	70	2095	mm	(island)

Column T
Temperatures: Highest/Lowest each year, on an average (−/ −)°C
Rainfall: Annual Total underlined (mm)

Alternative Spellings

Place Names

(Pinyin *left*; Traditional *right*)

Provinces and ARs

Anhui	Anhwei
Fujian	Fukien
Gansu	Kansu
Guangdong	Kwangtung
Guangxi Zhuang	Kwangsi Chuang
Guizhou	Kweichow
Hebei	Hopei
Heilongjiang	Heilungkiang
Hubei	Hupei
Hunan	Hunan
Liaoning	Liaoning
Nei Mongol	Inner Mongolia
Ningxia Huizu	Ningsia Hui
Qinghai	Tsinghai
Shaanxi	Shensi
Shandong	Shantung
Shanxi	Shansi
Sichuan	Szechwan
Taiwan	Taiwan
Xinjiang Uygur	Sinkiang Uighur
Xizang	Tibet
Yunnan	Yunnan
Zhejiang	Chekiang

Towns and Cities

Baotou	Paotow
Beijing	Peking
Benxi	Penki
Chengdu	Chengtu
Chongqing	Chungking
Dagang	Takang
Dagu	Taiku
Dalian	Talien
Daqing	Taching
Datong	Tatung
Daye	Tayeh
Dazhai	Tachai
Fuzhou	Foochow
Gaoxiong	Kaohsiung
Guangzhou	Canton
Guilin	Kweilin
Guiyang	Kweiyang
Hangzhou	Hangchow
Hohhot	Huehot
Huainan	Hwainan
Huangpu	Whampoa
Kashi	Kashgar
Kelamayi	Karamai
Jilin	Kirin
Jinan	Tsinan
Lanzhou	Lanchow
Luda	Luta
Luoyang	Loyang
Nanjing	Nanking
Ningbo	Ningpo
Qiqihar	Tsitsihar
Qinghuangdao	Chinwangtao
Qingdao	Tsingtao
Shanglie	Shengli
Shantou	Swatow
Shijiazhuang	Shikiachwan
Suzhou	Soochow
Suoche	Yarkand
Taibei	Taipei
Tianjing	Tientsin
Tonghua	Tungwha
Turpan	Turfan
Urumqi	Urumchi
Wuxi	Wuhsi
Wuzhou	Wuchow
Xiamen	Amoy
Xian	Sian
Xigong	Tzukung
Xuanhua	Hsuanhua
Xuzhou	Suchow
Yanan	Yenan
Yichang	Ichang
Zhengzhou	Chengchow
Zibo	Tzepo

Inland Basins

Taklimakan Shamo	Taklamakan Desert
Junggar Pendi	Dzungaria Basin
Qaidam Pendi	Tsaidam Basin

Rivers

Bei jiang	Pei kiang
Chang jiang	Yangtze kiang
	(middle & lower)
Dadu He	Tatu Ho
Dong jiang	Tung jiang
Gan jiang	Kan jiang
Gui jiang	Kwei kiang
Hongshui He	Hungshui Ho
Huai He	Hwai Ho
Huang He	Hwang Ho
Huangpu	Whangpoo
Songhua jiang	Sungari kiang
Xi jiang	Si kiang
Xiang jiang	Siang kiang
Zangbo jiang	Tsangpo kiang
Zhu jiang	Chu jiang (Pearl R.)

A Guide to Meanings

river	jiang, he
water	shui
sea	hai
ocean	yang
lake, pool	hu, po
island	dao, yu
bay, gulf	wan
cape	jiao
harbour, port	gang, gangkou
canal	yunhe
Grand Canal	Da Yunhe
irrigation canal	qu, qudao
well	jing
spring	quan
reservoir	shuiku
province	sheng
prefecture	diqu
county	xian
city	shi
commune	gongshe
town, village	cunzhen
township	xiang, zhen
(administrative)	

mountain	shan
mountain range	shanling
hilly land	shandi
mountains	shanmai
peak	feng
pass	guan
plain	ping yuan
basin	pendi
plateau	gao yuan
desert	shamo
north	bei
south	nan
east	dong
west	xi
upper	shang
central	zhong
lower	xia
big	da
small	xiao
left	zuo
right	you
inner	nei
outer	wai

Points to Consider

Sections are inserted throughout the books which list a number of points to consider. These are intended to pinpoint topics for further thought and discussion. They are not questions of fact alone, for teachers may draw up questions and answers on the factual content for themselves. Some of the statements made, however, may be thought sufficiently controversial to encourage readers to consider their validity, and to look at wider implications – those dealing with the development of minority regions, for example.

Glossary

Abbreviations

AR	Autonomous Region
CCP	Chinese Communist Party
KMT	Kuomintang (Guomintang) Party
MTR	Mass Transit Railway (Hong Kong)
PLA	People's Liberation Army
PRC	People's Republic of China
SEZ	Special Economic Zone

Political Phrases

Cultural Revolution
a movement started by Mao Zedong in 1966 to use strict communist principles to remove inequalities throughout China

Four Modernisations
modernising industry, agriculture, defence, and science and technology

Great Leap Forward
a short-lived movement begun in 1958 to introduce new thinking and new institutions, including the People's Communes (which made for progress) and 'backyard' iron and steel production (which did not)

Responsibility System
(a) Individuals or groups of people make an official contract to produce a commodity and sell a quota to the state; they may sell the rest on the open market
(b) some manufacturing enterprises receive state targets, but no state funds; they may make profits, but are taxed on them

Walking on Two Legs
combining modern and traditional methods, and large-scale and small-scale production

Political-Social

commune, production brigade ⎫ defined on
work team, work point ⎬ pp. 50–53

paramedic
a local medical helper, trained in preventitive medicine and health procedures, using modern and traditional techniques

policy of egality
working so that all people and institutions have equal opportunities and rewards

quota
fixed share to be contributed or received

Political Terms

autonomous
self-governing

bureaucracy
government through officials

cadre (kanpu)
leader; official; person with above-average educational qualifications

dynasty
line of hereditary rulers

ethnic
of a particular race or cultural group

feudal system
in which a superior person holds absolute rights over subjects

foreign concession
an area of land placed under foreign control and justice

Han Chinese
general ethnic name for Chinese people, derived from the Han dynasty (206 BC–AD 220), when northern Chinese expanded over a wide empire

legation
residence of diplomatic minister

minority people
ethnic group of people other than Han Chinese, and smaller in numbers

serf (Russian origin)
labourer tied to the land, and sold with it

warlord
military governor commanding local troops

Industrial/Technical

artifact
product of human workmanship

biogas
inflammable gas (mainly methane) from organic waste

geothermal energy
derived from heat sources beneath the earth's surface

high technology
using up to date skills and modern scientific methods to make sophisticated machinery or other products

hydraulic cannon
a machine projecting high-powered water jets

intermediate technology
skillful use of simple methods and available materials to make efficient machinery or other products

processing plant
machinery which converts raw materials to usable form

seismograph
instrument for detecting an earthquake and recording information about it

sluice-gate
sliding gate to adjust an opening through which water is channelled

solar energy
that which emanates from the sun

tamping
beating down material between enclosing walls

Urban

conurbation
continuous urban area formed by the expansion of neighbouring towns (may include some open land)

hutong
a narrow road, or lane, between houses near the city centre (as in Beijing)

neighbourhood committee
non-governmental group, selected by and from residents, which gives community service, with a small reward from local government

satellite town
a separate town within a metropolitan area, or close to a city, but separated by rural land from the main urban settlement

'snowball effect' (applied to a town)
a continuous increase in size as more functions bring in more people and encourage other functions, which do the same

Physical Conditions and Vegetation

alluvial fan
material deposited and spread fan-like by a stream, whose flow slackens as it emerges from a steeper valley to a plain of gentler gradient

alluvium
water-borne material deposited on a surface

aspect
the direction a surface faces and how it is angled in relation to the sun and wind

calcareous
containing calcium carbonate

deciduous
seasonal leaf-shedding

distributary
one of the streams of a branching river which distributes part of the main flow, as in a delta

dyke
ridge built to prevent a river flooding adjacent low-lying land: in places dykes are natural levées, built-up and strengthened

fault-bounded (face)
steep rock slope following the line of a fault, along which the lower surface it overlooks has been vertically displaced

kaoliang
a tall millet, up to 2 m high, with a purple flower head; used for food and fodder; can be grown in quite dry areas

karst
limestone country, with surface joints widened by solution, vertical shafts, and underground drainage: collapse and further solution may leave pinnacles and blocks

loamy soil
clay mixed with coarser particles (silt and sand) to form a permeable, friable soil

loess
  accumulation of fine wind-borne particles, which tend to adhere to one another
monsoon wind
  seasonal airflow caused by temperature variation between a land surface and the adjacent ocean. Used where the summer wind direction is the reverse of that in winter
organic waste
  associated with living matter and left to decompose
river capture
  a river changes direction to flow through a valley, which another river has eroded back and so undercut it
secondary woodland
  vegetation whose trees and shrubs have replaced the original forest plants
silt
  very fine particles: larger than clay particles, but smaller than sand
steppe
  treeless plain with grasses and other herbs: tends to be dry

Miscellaneous

acupuncture
  the use of metal needles to puncture parts of the body to relieve pain and cure various conditions: an ancient practice still widely used
blood fluke
  minute parasitic worm carried in the blood
ceramic
  connected with pottery
joss stick
  fragrant stick for incense
paddy
  (*padi*-Malay) describes rice grown under wet conditions
pictograph
  written character which conveys the idea not the sound, and may be used for different dialects
Tai Ji Quan
  a form of callisthenics (exercise) involving meditation in movement
terra cotta
  hard brownish pottery

References and Further Reading

Needham, J., (abridged Ronan, C.A.) *Science and Civilisation in China*, C.U.P., 1978

Fitzgerald, P., *Ancient China*, Elsevier-Phaidon, 1978

Nancarrow, P., *Early China and the Wall*, C.U.P., 1978

Topping, A., China's Incredible Find (Buried Army), *Nat. Geog. Mag.*, 153 (4), p.440, 1980

Geog. Mag., (ed.), Army of Clay Comes Out of Hiding, *Geog. Mag.*, LIII(3), p.196 (1980)

Nelson, H., Maps from Old Cathay, *Geog Mag.* XLVII(11), p.702 (1975)

Kahn-Ackermann, M., *China – Within the Outer Gate*, Marco Polo Press, 1982

Money, D.C., *China Today*, C.U.P., 1987

Cannon, T., Jenkins, A., Modern China – Changes After Mao, *Geog. Mag.* LVIII(10), p.506 (1986)

Doak Barnett, A., *China's Economy in Global Perspective*, The Brookings Institute, Washington, D.C., 1981

Jackson, S.H., Population Policy in the People's Republic of China, *Geography* 66 (3) p.235 (1981)

Sartaj Aziz, *Rural Development – Learning from China*, Macmillan, 1978

Corrigan, P., Ping Chow – A Chinese Commune, *Geography* 62 (2), p.125 (1977)

Leeming, F., Powell, S., Behind the Open Door (Rural Organisation), *Geog. Mag.* LVIII (9) p.457 (1986)

Cannon, T., Jenkins, A., The Chinese Socialist Experience, *Geography* 72 (4), p.335 (1987)

Pannell, C.W., *China: The Geography of Development and Modernisation*, Arnold & Winston 1983

Watson, A., The Reform of Agricultural Marketing in China since 1978, *The China Quarterly*, 113, p.1 (1988)

Cannon, T., Jenkins, A., Freeing the Market Forces, *Geog. Mag.* LVIII (11), p.566 (1986)

Cannon, T., Jenkins, A., A Country So Changed, *Geography* 71 (4), p.343 (1986)

Cole, J.P., *China 1950–2000: Performance and Prospects* (Univ. of Nottingham) 1985

Macmillan, W., Lost and Found – A Sense of China, *Geog. Review* Vol.1 (5), p.8 (1988)

Kirkby, R., China – The Altering face of Urbanisation, *Geog. Mag.* LVIII (10), p.508 (1986)

Phillips, D.R., Oil in Chinese Waters, *Geog. Mag.* LVI (9), p.444 (1984)

van Buren, A., (ed) *The Chinese Biogas Manual*, Intermediate Technology Publications

Phillips, D.R., The Shenzhen Special Economic Zone, *Geography* 68(4), p.289 (1983)

Hardill, I., The Shenzhen Experiment, *Geography* 71 (2), p.146 (1986)

Phillips, D.R., Hong Kong Border-Line, *Geog. Mag.* LVII (3), p.114 (1985)

King, O.P., Beijing, *Geog. Mag.* LII (5), p.359 (1980)

Dwyer, D.J., Chengdu, Sichuan: Modernisation of a Chinese City, *Geography* 71 (3), p.215 (1986)

Dale, B., Shanghai, *Nat. Geog. Mag.* 158 (1), p.2 (1980)

Pask, R., North-East China Transformed, *Geog. Mag.* LIII (1), p.53 (1980)

Derbyshire, E., Environmental Change: The Record in the Loess along the Old Silk Road, *Geography* 69 (2), p.108 (1984)

Waltham, T., Smart, P., Under China's Karstlands, *Geog. Mag.* LVIII (4), p.117 (1986)

Sweeting, M.M., Intricacies of Chinese Karst, *Geog. Mag.* LII (4), p.306 (1980)

Sweeting, M.M., The Karst of Sweilin (Guilin), *Geog. Journ.* 144 (2), p.199 (1978)

Sweeting, M.M., The Landscape of One-Seventh of China, *Geog. Mag.* L. (6), p.393 (1978)

Zhang Zhiyi, Old Formations in a Young Republic, *Geog. Mag.* LII (2), p.89 (1979)

Gregory, K., China's Rivers, *Geog. Journ.*, 144 (2), p.194 (1978)

Da Guang, Chinese Discover Chang jiang Source, *Geog. Mag.* LI (10), p.665 (1979)

Waltham, T., Through the Heart of China (Chang jiang gorges) *Geog. Mag.* LVII (11), p.619 (1985)

Ting Yi-Lan, Water is the Chinese Life Force, *Geog. Mag.* LII (4), p.257 (1980)

Walling, D.E., Yellow River, Which Never Runs Clear, *Geog. Mag.* LIII (9), p.568 (1981)

Liu Changning; Linag Jiyang, China's Sorrow – Huang He, *Geog. Mag.* LIX (2), p.41 (1987)

Griffiths, E., China Develops the West, *Geog. Mag*, L (7), p.457 (1978)

Gore, R., Journey to China's Far West, *Nat. Geog. Mag.* 157 (3), p.292 (1980)

Allen, P., Inside Chinese Tibet, *Geog. Mag.* LII (12), p.830 (1980)

Maxwell, B., Desalinated Water for Thirsty Hong Kong, *Geog. Mag.* LIII (2), p.452 (1976)

Phillips, D.R., New Towns Bring New Hope for Expanding Hong Kong, *Geog. Mag.* LIII (3), p.180 (1980)

Mountjoy, A.B., Housing in New Towns in Hong Kong, *Geography* 65 (1), p.53 (1980)

Phillips, D.R., Hong Kong: Edging Towards Local Democracy, *Geography* 71(2), p.142 (1986)

Drakakis-Smith, D.W., Portugal on the Chinese frontier (Macao), *Geog. Mag.* XLVII (1), p.676 (1975)

Grove, N., Taiwan Confronts a New Era, *Nat. Geog. Mag.* 161 (1), p.92 (1982)

Periodicals

Encyclopedia of New China ed. Luo Liang et al. (Foreign Languages Press, Beijing)

The China Quarterly (School of Oriental and African Studies, London)

China Official Annual Report (Kingsway International Publications)

China Reconstructs (The Chinese Welfare Institute, Beijing)

China Now (The Society for Anglo-Chinese Understanding, London)

Social Sciences in China (Chinese Academy of Social Sciences, Beijing)

Beijing Review (Foreign Languages Press, Beijing)

China Daily (in English) (Xinhua News Agency, London)

China's Foreign Trade (China Publications Centre, Beijing)

China Pictorial (China Publications Centre, Beijing)

Economic Reporter (Economic Information Agency, Hong Kong)

Agency: Collets (Subscription Import Department), Denington Estate, Wellingborough, Northants NN8 2QT

Place name index

General index